PAINTBOXED!

PAINTBOXED!

Introduction by
Bob English

Paul Jodard

PAINTBOXED!

B.T. Batsford Ltd, London

PAINTING		paint	wash	shade		magnify	zoom	DRAW STEN		USE STENCIL	
GRAPHICS		chalk	copy	smudge		Quantel Paintbox		save picsten		display sten	
EFFECTS		airbrush	restore	smooth				old	new	reverse sten	
PASTEUP	3D		crisp	blur					wipe pic	USE	GRID
ANIMATION			field	1	2			restore pic			

Author's acknowledgements

The idea for this book began in conversations with Roger Thornton some years ago, and I have a debt of thanks to him and his colleagues at Quantel, especially Bob Pank, for help and encouragement while the work was being done. I've also enjoyed talking to Paintbox users around the world, and I'm grateful to them for the enthusiasm they showed for this book.

Particular thanks go to Bob English for providing an introduction, and to Kim Mannes-Abbott for the jacket image.

The terms Quantel, Paintbox, Hal, Henry, Harriet, Picturebox, Cypher and Domino are protected trade names of Quantel Ltd., Turnpike Rd., Newbury, Berkshire.

© Paul Jodard 1993
First published 1993
Introduction © Bob English, 1993
Conclusion © Bob Pank, 1993

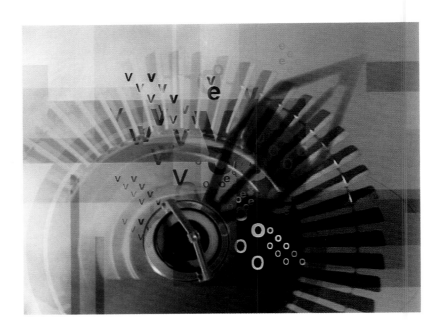

Cover image by Kim Mannes-Abbott
Designed by the Armelle Press
Typeset by MetraDisc
Printed in Singapore

for the publishers
B.T.Batsford Ltd
4 Fitzhardinge Street
London W1H 0AH
ISBN 0 7134 7293 6

A CIP catalogue record for this book is available from the British Library

Contents

Introduction *Bob English* 7

The Post-Modern Machine *Paul Jodard* 11

The Best Electronic Images 45

Paintbox — The Future *Bob Pank* 131

Index 143

Most of you reading this long-awaited book will probably take the Paintbox for granted – it does seem to have been around for a long time. However, only a decade ago – back in the dark ages of television design – things were done very differently or not at all.

The most telling changes have taken place in the area of news and current affairs. Ten years ago, graphics were produced on twelve by nine inch captions as stills for the studio camera, or, more lavishly, a pull caption would be used to create animated effects. If time allowed, the designer might just about be able to produce a film sequence. This required enormous skill and judgment and often a lot of luck. A re-shoot even for the simplest mistake would be out of the question given the almost impossible deadlines. The graphics studios of those days would look positively Dickensian to today's designers. I remember once visiting a current affairs graphics area (one that shall remain nameless) and being rooted to the spot, unable to move – the entire floor was coated in aerosol spray glue!

All this provides the backdrop to the arrival of Flair. The year would be 1981 and the machine arrived with much fanfare. It was an early prototype, jointly developed by Logica and the BBC's Kingswood Warren, and we, the BBC designers, were to be the guinea pigs putting it through its paces. To be truthful, most of us were a little afraid of exposing our limitations in full view of everyone. This, I think, would be my first encounter with what could be called 'techno-fear'. I wasn't alone in feeling threatened. It seemed odd then to be looking at a screen rather than at your hand, something everyone now considers to be perfectly natural. This early machine seemed to suit better the more naturally gifted illustrator, rather than the designer, and I remember seeing some excellent early work by Graham McCallum – my own efforts seemed pathetic in comparison.

Shortly after Flair arrived, I left the BBC to join Channel Four, the newly established

INTRODUCTION BY BOB ENGLISH

The work illustrated here was chosen by Bob English from his extensive portfolio of Paintbox images. The final image is from the Credit Agricole commercial mentioned in the text.

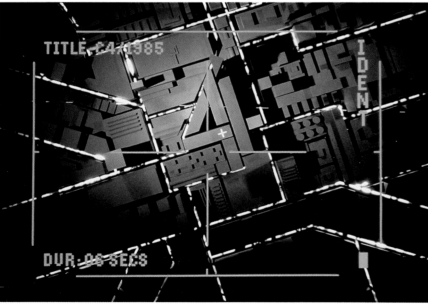

British commercial arts channel, to set up a new graphic department there. It had just three inmates, myself, Simon Broom and a spanking brand-new Paintbox – the first one to be installed in a television station! The only problem was that the Paintbox was so new nobody quite knew where it should go, and so for six months it quietly occupied a broom cupboard. But at least this delay gave me a chance to learn how the system worked and to overcome my techno-fear. Both Simon and I produced some very creditable efforts on behalf of Channel Four, and the promotional slide (in Paintbox form at least) was born!

Having been thrust into the forefront of the technology, I was asked, along with two other designers, by Quantel, the makers of Paintbox, to put the machine through its paces for a promotional video that they were making. The company set a fictitious project concerning the events surrounding the American War of Independence (an eye to export sales here!) We were given the brief and a deadline and told to get on with it. I cringe with embarrassment whenever I am unfortunate enough to see this video. However it was clear even then that the impact of Paintbox on the design profession would be profound. Paintbox has undoubtedly promoted designers, and made them far more visible to a wider range of people. Generally, the 1980s were a boom time for design anyway, but television design exploded, and while Paintbox wasn't the only reason, it was certainly very influential. The real power of Paintbox has since been tapped by many different types of client, from photo fits for the police to retouching and repairing commercials. As a stand-alone machine, it has limitations but its real potential is harnessed when linked to the Quantel Harry and later when used in Henry. Much of the work I am currently involved in utilizes Paintbox in some form or another. At the inception of a project I will often use Paintbox to create a visual indication to a client of how a job may eventually look. In common with other designer-directors, I use

Harry or Henry to combine elements that I
would have previously prepared. These can be
as many and varied as live action, computer
graphics, traditional animation, model shoots
and typography. A recent commercial
completed for FCB in Paris involved direct-
ing aerial shots from a helicopter at various
locations around France and then combining
this material with computer-generated
typography, matching frame for frame every
move – who said design was boring!

Of course, none of this exciting technology
would be of any value if it wasn't for the
many talented designers and illustrators who
use this equipment much as though they were
sitting at a drawing board. This is one of the
main strengths of Paintbox. It has been
developed with input from a designer, and we
can all thank Martin Holbrook, ex-Quantel,
who was hugely responsible for making sure
that the machine could be used by a designer
and that it wasn't necessary to have a science
degree to operate one.

This book will be a great opportunity to
see for yourselves the quality of work produced from around the world. Like every-
thing in life, you get out what you put in and
fortunately Paintbox rewards those blessed
with talent and is unkind to the lesser
mortals. Judge for yourselves. Happy browsing!

The Quantel Paintbox,
ready for use.

Paul Jodard

Some time ago I had to go to Venice, a city I hadn't visited in over a decade, to discuss an exhibition for a New York arts centre. I'd booked into a modest hotel on the Giudecca, and was looking forward to seeing Venice again. But as the plane began its final approach I was seized by a moment of utter panic. How, in a city with 'streets full of water', as I had been advised, could I get a taxi to take me to my hotel? Could I even walk to the Giudecca, without getting my feet wet? A few second's reflection recalled to mind the vaporetto, and changed my mood from panic to anticipated pleasure.

I recalled this panic, and hit a similar one when I was first invited to use a Paintbox. Where, my first thought was, have they put the keyboard? While I'm long used to facing a screen every day, and even to pointing and shooting with a mouse and pad, how was it going to be possible to communicate with this machine without a keyboard? Even the pen I had been handed seemed far too insignificant an object, compared to the friendly litter of rulers, compasses, pencils, tape and clips to be found on my drawing board.

Half an hour later the slim grey pen seemed a quite natural means of dealing with the machine, and I was using it not only to add elements to the design in different ways, but also to flick on and off the different menus and palettes, as if I had been doing so for ages. It seemed a quite natural gesture, compared to pushing a mouse around a pad, which is a technique that while familiar still feels artificial. A moment's thought showed this distinction to be an odd one, and I tried to work out what it might mean, for in truth both sets of movements represent a man-machine interface via a screen, both have to be learnt, and both depend on similar hand and eye co-ordination. Yet the one with a pen felt 'natural' and the other – the more familiar mouse – 'artificial'. There are, of course, hardware differences. The mouse is physically attached to the machine, and so the cord does act as a constraint on movement, simply because the user knows it is there. A trackball feels less restrained, but still slightly odd, while the way a pen is held like a conventional pen or brush is also familiar

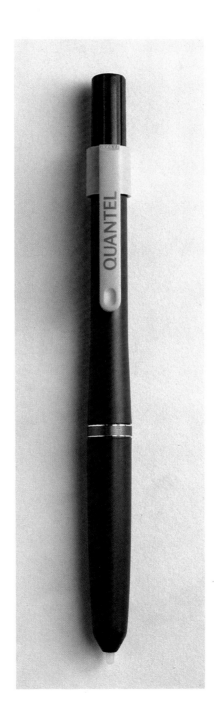

The pen used with the Paintbox, full size.

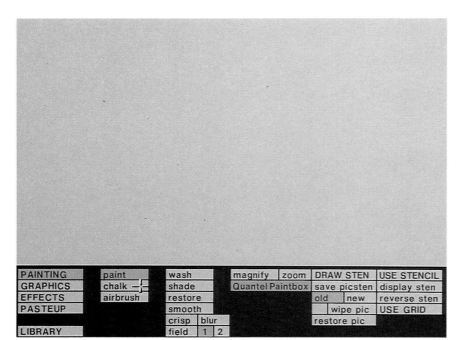

The Paintbox screen, ready for use. Below, images created by Paula Maras of Quantel to promote Cypher.

from childhood. The fact that the reaction time of the Paintbox was effectively zero, compared to the perceptibly longer delay on conventional computers (even fast ones) was also clearly important: it seemed possible to pile ideas and changes on to the screen as fast as the pen would move, unlike the tap-and-wait or mouse-and-pause of some graphics systems I had used. But I felt there was more to it than simply a familiar hand position and a faster chip in the box. Quantel had in some way produced a means of communicating with their machine of a new order, breaking free from the traditional hegemony of the keyboard. To explain this better let us look at the principal features of the Paintbox system, and how it works.

To understand what a Paintbox does, it is necessary to look back over the history of the system. The first Paintbox, now called the Classic Paintbox, was introduced in 1982 as a design aid for television use. It was created in response to a perceived need for television programme makers to handle images and graphics directly in a compatible system, without using film or still cameras or pre-printed material to provide originals. In this context the Paintbox became rapidly popular with TV news departments, with graphics departments in television, and with design companies working with TV advertising. Its ability to make or manipulate images on screen without necessarily drawing on other technologies was a key factor, as was the user-friendliness of the system, its speed of handling and its image quality.

In 1989 the system underwent a major re-design, with the introduction of the Paintbox V series, in which the previous standard circuitry was replaced with custom-designed circuit boards. These dedicated circuit boards not only saved weight and energy but also processing time. The increased speed of processing chips and the availability of cheaper (and larger) memory is a commonplace of modern computer technology, but it should not be overlooked that often an incremental step in technology can unlock a whole range of new applications. Higher speeds in processing and greater memory available increased exponentially the range of the Paintbox – for example in 1985 an add-on storage system allowed up to 80 television 'frames' to be held in disc. Today the current magneto-optical discs are not only a quarter of the size and weight of the previous system but allow for up to 700 pictures, which can be stored and retrieved much more rapidly. To describe the Quantel Paintbox only in the same terms as computers is not strictly accurate either: the Paintbox is not just a software programme, but integrated hardware and software, in which the strictly computing element is secondary, in fact, to image handling. It has therefore been possible to design the Paintbox to avoid the problems that can be encountered with purely software-based programmes for computer graphics (particularly in terms of scale, colour rendition and perspective). In the same way the Paintbox should not be seen only as a stand-alone machine, but as a common element in a variety of machines designed for specific applications, in graphics, video or television design. All these machines are as compatible as possible, and, in keeping with the multiple-approach of the on-screen techniques, as we shall see, configurations are not fixed immovably – indeed interfaces exist to link the Paintbox with an increasing range of other input and output equipment, and with other imaging systems.

From the basic Paintbox of 1982 a range of machines has developed. These include the Harry and Harriet editing suites, designed to handle increasing numbers of television images, and to edit live over live video in real time. When a news programme shows a state meeting in place over the shoulder of the newscaster sitting in his studio, or a sports event is televised with the clock counting the athletes' times on screen, a Paintbox has probably been used to prepare and play back in real time these effects. Harriet, in addition, has facilities for animation, and both systems can be linked to Cypher, a high-performance effects program which generates three dimensional movement effects for graphics or stills, rotating, tumbling and zooming them on screen. The Picturebox was also introduced as an image

The Hal (top), Henry (middle) and new Micro Henry systems all use a Paintbox as part of a wider range of functions.

store, to and from which images could be passed by the Video Paintbox itself, or by the Paintbox systems in Harry and Harriet. The most recent additions to the television and video range are Hal and Henry, both

Basic operations: pressing the pen towards the menu area creates the cursor, and fixes the operation required: here a 70 percent airbrush effect (top). Freehand movement with the pen across the tablet creates marks, intensity differing according to pressure. Colours can be selected and mixed in the palette (middle). Simple shapes can be created using the 'geometry set,' filled with colour and highlighted in airbrush to give an effect of depth.

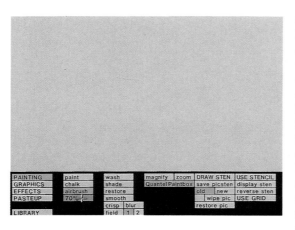

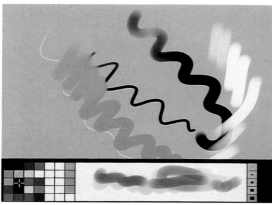

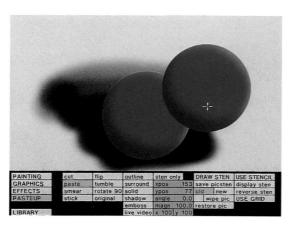

introduced in 1992. Hal is a compositing system, able to create and assemble multi-layered video images, while Henry is an editing system, with fifteen minutes of real time memory, and a full range of edit suite

facilities, which include image and graphic handling, and rotoscoping and other visual effects. Both systems can layer live on live video, and replay in real time. In a new departure Quantel unveiled Domino at the end of 1992, a system (Digital Opticals for Movies), that brings the same high quality image treatment available for graphics and television to the motion picture industry. By scanning film images into the system, Domino allows the movie-maker the same range of facilities for special effects as available to the television producer, with the simplicity of working through a single system.

On the graphics side, the Graphics Paintbox offers a range of techniques for painting, editing and enhancing graphic images, whether produced on-screen or developed from input images. The range of colours available and the screen definition exceed much of the best computer graphics software, and the increasing demand for images of such quality led to the introduction of the Desktop Paintbox, specifically designed to interface with the Apple Macintosh. Using Desktop a designer on Mac can grab images created on Mac into the Paintbox, edit them using the range of Paintbox functions and output them via the Mac.

Whatever the intended application, the basic elements of the Paintbox from where the designer sits are the screen, tablèt and pen, plus input and output devices. Depending on the task – for example whether the machine is for graphic, television or now film work – the configuration of these devices will differ slightly, as will the ancillary equipment such as hand units or keypads available. The central element functions in much the same in all cases, from the user's point of view, though command menus and structures may differ according to the intended task. In all cases the machine can be used to start up a design process from cold, in other words by treating the screen as a blank sheet of paper or film, or the machine can be used to develop or reconfigure images created in other media. And, of course, machine-created images can be combined with others. This versatility is a key factor, not only because of the range of different images that can be input into the system, but also in the fact that all input is treated equally: there are no hierarchies on screen. (Traditional photo-retouching, for example, works by an additive-only process: the original print is a base to which material is added by airbrush or mask. In Paintbox the original print becomes a digitized image which can be manipulated in any way the operator chooses.) The process of combination of images is equally hierarchy-free: designs created on screen can be merged with externally-gathered images at any time in the process, and the 'rules of engagement' are completely open (unlike many so-called Desk-top publishing programmes, under which areas of the screen have to be specifically allocated either as picture or text boxes). Given the large storage facilities available, images can be stored at regular stages in their development, allowing the designer to 'backtrack' to make changes easily. Images can be presented to the client on Paintbox without being committed to an output system, thereby keeping design options open for as late as possible in the design process.

The basic elements of pen, screen and tablet have been mentioned: the typical Paintbox screen is about 500 mm on the diagonal (though any size of screen could be fitted to the system), with a tablet about two-thirds of the size, while the pen is the same size as a fountain pen. In a normal working configuration the operator's hand sits over the tablet, while the screen fills the field of vision without crowding it. Bringing the pen near the surface of the tablet makes a cursor appear, while pressing on the tablet with the pen creates a mark on the screen. The form and colour of marks created by the pen are defined by the instruction menus, which can be called up by flicking the pen across the left or right edge of the tablet. This movement, called 'swiping' also can be used to call up the colour palette, by swiping across the top or bottom edges of the tablet. The tablet is blank, and has no marking on it, and the artist works always looking at the

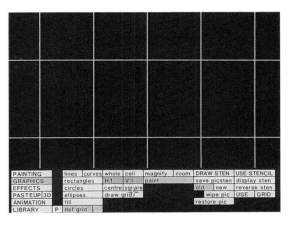

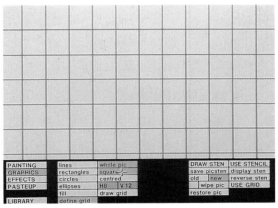

Grids can be drawn using the graphics box. Here two alternative grids are stored under the old and new boxes. Type (bottom) can be imported from fonts in memory, and scaled, sized, spaced and coloured at will on screen.

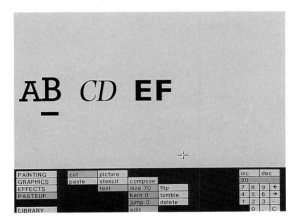

screen, not at the hands. Because of the immediate response of the cursor or image on screen to pen movements, the hand-eye co-ordination develops rapidly, and as I myself found, quickly seems quite natural.

The colour palette is laid out like a watercolour box, with 'pots' of colour to one side and a central mixing area, in which colours from the pots can be mixed and overlaid, as well as picking and using colours from the screen (for example from existing images) added. The size of the brush (and whether it works as paintbrush, airbrush or chalk) can also be defined from the palette. Any pot on the palette can also be filled with mixed colours, or colours from the screen. This is done by pressing down on the chosen colour to 'load' the pen (a bar on the right of the palette indicates the current pen colour), and then pressing it again onto the paintpot or mixing area. Paint can be overlaid on screen and in the mixing area. Since the pen is pressure sensitive, a light stroke deposits a thin film of paint, and using more pressure deposits more paint, up to one hundred percent opacity. As the paint is otherwise transparent, different densities create mixes with background colours. Thus precise tonal variations can be achieved and taken up by the pen for use as brush colours. The Paintbox (unlike some graphics programmes) does not have a fixed range of predetermined colours. There is an upper limit of 16,277,216 colours, or two to the power of twenty-four − the product of three channels of 8-bit wide information.

The menus are displayed with the six major functions listed down the left column in grey boxes. Tapping the pen on a menu box selects it, turning it pink, and prompting the display of relevant sub-menus on the right of the box. For example, selecting the major menu Painting calls up the choice of paint, chalk and airbrush as paint styles. Selecting airbrush from this sub-menu brings up a new box for adjusting the flow rate of the airbrush. In every case only the functions relevant to the current operation are shown, so keeping the displays clear and uncluttered. Curiously, the two menu colours, grey and pink, were very fashionable with designers at the time the Graphics Paintbox first became widely available, but which came first is an unanswerable question.

Different stages and applications in the creation of a design call up different menus,

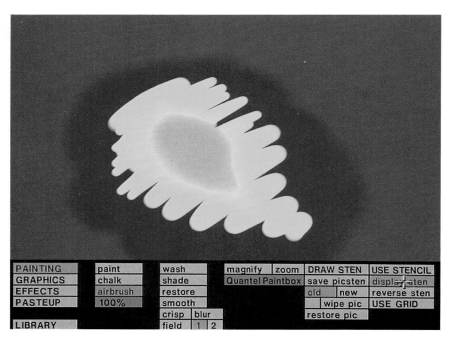

PAINTING	paint	wash		magnify	zoom	DRAW STEN	USE STENCIL
GRAPHICS	chalk	shade		Quantel Paintbox		save picsten	display sten
EFFECTS	airbrush	restore				old	new	reverse sten
PASTEUP	100%	smooth					wipe pic	USE GRID
		crisp	blur			restore pic	
LIBRARY		field	1	2			

The stencil technique (top) is of great importance, and so is a feature of most menus. Red is used as a standard colour for stencils (following darkroom practice, but any colour can be used.) Once a stencil image has been created (middle) it can be pasted repeatedly onto the image (bottom). A variety of shadow and relief effects can be applied to such images.

Opposite

The copy brush (top) lifts pixels from one end of a rectangular grid and deposits them at the other. This can be used for retouching, for extending backgrounds, and for repeating areas of an image. The smear effect spreads the edge of an image in the direction of pen movement, to create speed and movement effects (below).

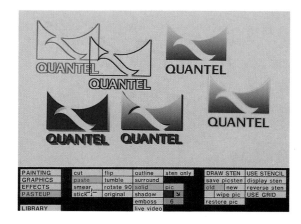

PAINTING	cut	flip	outline	sten only	DRAW STEN	USE STENCIL
GRAPHICS	paste	tumble	surround		save picsten	display sten
EFFECTS	smear	rotate 90	solid	pic	old	new	reverse sten
PASTEUP	stick	original	shadow		wipe pic	USE GRID
			emboss	6	restore pic	
LIBRARY			live video			

but there are various common features. Firstly, all menus provide a means of saving work in progress through the use of the two boxes labelled Old and New (these are so called to differentiate the boxes: no hierarchy or priority is suggested by them). This is separate from the storage facilities of the system library. Each menu box provides constant access to adjacent menus, and entry to any other major menu is only a pen-tap away. One feature, the stencil menu, was originally one of a number of available boxes, but it was soon realized how important stencil was, for masking and cutting out images, and its centrality to so many operations was recognised by including the stencil box on all menus, so that stencil could be directly accessed at any time.

A further common feature is the frequent provision of several alternative ways of achieving a desired result. For example, although the Paintbox is a pure digital machine there are few occasions when numbers need to be used by the operator. When numbers are needed two methods are usually provided for setting them. A number pad appears on the menu screen, and numbers can be tapped individually, or the pen can be moved over the picture area to increase (up and right) or decrease (down and left) number values. So, to set the flow rate for airbrush (expressed as a percentage), a number pad appears when the pen is tapped on the density box. Individual numerals can be picked out by the pen, and transferred to the box, or the keypad can be used, or the increment/decrement boxes on screen or keypad can be used to adjust the existing percentage up or down. Finally, the density can be changed by moving the pen over the screen area, while the menu is on, until the required figure reads out . This multiplicity of choice is deliberate, and indeed one of the fundamentals of the Paintbox. The system designer's intention was to create as free-form a working environment as possible, and this extended from the simplest to the most complex operations. The thought behind this was that the machines should be operated by designers, not computer experts, and that

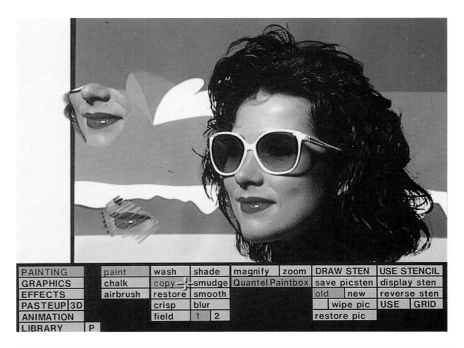

PAINTING		paint	wash	shade	magnify	zoom	DRAW STEN	USE STENCIL
GRAPHICS		chalk	copy	smudge	Quantel Paintbox		save picsten	display sten
EFFECTS		airbrush	restore	smooth			old	new	reverse sten
PASTEUP	3D		crisp	blur				wipe pic	USE	GRID
ANIMATION			field	1	2			restore pic	
LIBRARY	P							

PAINTING		paint	wash	shade	magnify	zoom	DRAW STEN	USE STENCIL
GRAPHICS		chalk	copy	smudge	Quantel Paintbox		save picsten	display sten
EFFECTS		airbrush	restore	smooth			old	new	reverse sten
PASTEUP	3D	100%	crisp	blur				wipe pic	USE	GRID
ANIMATION			field	1	2			restore pic	
LIBRARY	P							

since designers work in different ways, and approach problems through differing techniques, a machine intended as a design tool should be as flexible as possible, and respond to different working methods.

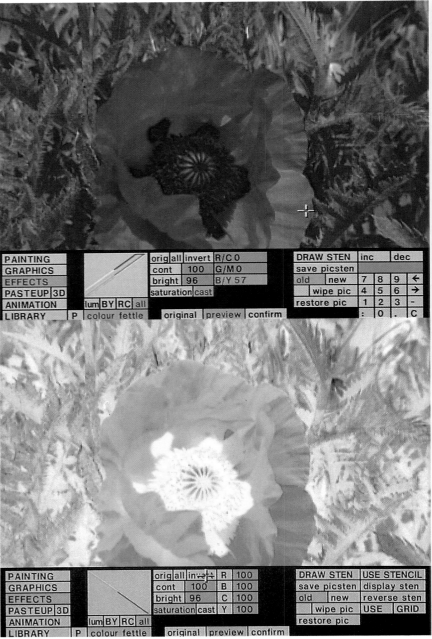

A second image can be stored 'below' the first, and brushed through. This layering effect is used to create the sky in the middle picture. A colour wash can be laid over a whole image (bottom picture) which will retain the luminance values of the original. A more sophisticated colour handling technique is fettle (above right). This allows the operator to alter the colour values of a whole image. The starting values are displayed as a set of four colour profiles in the menu box, which can be changed either by 'pulling' on the lines with the pen, or by rewriting values numerically.

Similarly, the designer should be able to operate the machine with a minimum of learning time, and work in a way that leaves energy free for creativity, not tying it up with remembering programme routines and commands. Of course, operating a top-end editing suite such as Henry demands a level of technical knowledge, but even there the working system is organized so that the operator can perform virtually all tasks with screen, pen and tablet only.

Turning to what the Paintbox can do, first and foremost, as the name implies, it can be used to paint. Using either a paint brush, chalk or airbrush, and any one of the myriad colours that can be created on the palette, the artist can draw freehand or use the set of drawing instruments for lines, circles, squares and ellipses contained in Paintbox. Chosen areas of the image can be filled with a solid colour, or a colour graduated between two tints. Stencils can be cut and used to mask and re-colour areas of the image. Lines and areas of images can be sharpened, blurred or spread using the smooth, crisp and smear controls. Patches of colour, or whole images, can be copied from one area to another, either using the copy brush or by creating and sticking cutouts. Type can be added, tinted and coloured, and shadow, relief and background effects generated for type matter and images. The colour of an image can be varied both in terms of colour balance and luminance. These techniques can be applied to freehand drawn images, or images grabbed onto the screen from other sources: still photos, video images, drawings, scanned type, or whatever. Once in the system's library, these images can be cut out, re-sized, and re-assembled with other images, and manipulated in space to produce three-dimensional effects.In the video applications of Paintbox, images can be animated in real time, to generate an enormously complex series of effects. These images can be combined and output as stills, video and, most recently, as 35mm film.

To look at each technique in the above catalogue independently would be to overlook one of the main qualities of the Paintbox, its ability to combine different techniques seamlessly into the same image. The examples of different techniques that follow should be seen as highlighting particular aspects of the Paintbox's arsenal, rather than identifying them uniquely.

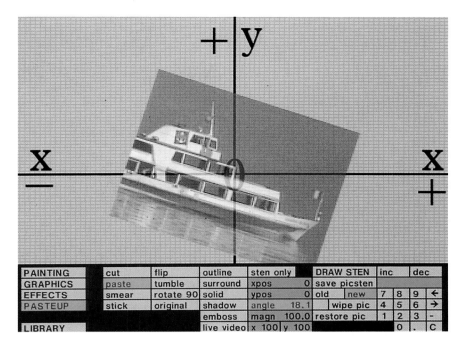

PAINTING	cut	flip	outline	sten only	DRAW STEN	inc	dec
GRAPHICS	paste	tumble	surround	xpos	0	save picsten	
EFFECTS	smear	rotate 90	solid	ypos	0	old	new	7	8	9	←
PASTEUP	stick	original	shadow	angle	18.1	wipe pic	4	5	6	→
			emboss	magn	100.0	restore pic	1	2	3	-
LIBRARY			live video	x 100	y 100		0	.	C

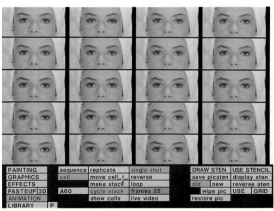

PAINTING	sequence	replicate	single shot	DRAW STEN	USE STENCIL
GRAPHICS	cell	move cell	reverse	save picsten	display sten
EFFECTS		make stack	loop	old	new	reverse sten
PASTEUP 3D	A60	cycle stack	frames 25	wipe pic	USE	GRID
ANIMATION		show cells	live video	restore pic	
LIBRARY	P				

Images can be rotated through three planes. The centre point of the axes of movement can be placed anywhere on the screen (top) and these effects animated into a sequence of images.
Animation effects can also be created by modifying and repeating images as with traditional overlay animation (middle). By layering video sequences and using stencils, images can be made to pass through each other during animation sequences.
Selected images can be stored in the library, either within the Paintbox or on an external store (such as a Picturebox) or on removable magneto-optical disc.

PAINTING	find	fetch	titles	DRAW STEN	USE STENCIL
GRAPHICS	save	delete	browse	save picsten	display sten
EFFECTS	directory	archive		old	new	reverse sten
PASTEUP	def group	overlay	down	wipe pic	USE GRID
				restore pic	
LIBRARY	picture	TRAINING TAPE IMAGES - 033	

FREEHAND DRAWING

Scott Harding's Centaur, created entirely on Paintbox.
Sam Madragona's Nu Shooz cover, before and after (below).
'Bird's Eye View' by Mary Webb (above, right).
Steve Canvin's 'Churchill on Paintbox' (below, right).

As we have already seen, the basic Paintbox element is the set of brushes and colour palette for freehand drawing. Almost any Paintboxed image will have an element of drawing in it, and some are built up completely on screen, with or without an external image as a guide, and without such a guide image being scanned in to provide a basis for further drawing. Scott Harding of Grafx chose to create his image of the mythical centaur completely on Paintbox,

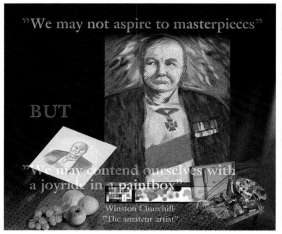

using some stencil effects to build up the cloud patterns. Mary Webb's *Bird's Eye View* was based on a photograph for the main image, but this was not scanned in, simply used as a guide. For an album cover for Nu Shooz, Sam Mandragona scanned in a monochrome photograph and drew over it in pen to highlight and extend the jacket, then used airbrush to put in the yellow background and the frames. A stencil was used to colour in the face, and a background texture input and tinted.

Steven Canvin, who works at Wiz-Art in Denmark, set out with his *Churchill in Paintbox* to 'show that the Graphic Paintbox can simulate traditional art.' The oil paint finish was created using the smear, shift, and chalk effects, and the canvas background created using embossing.

STENCILS AND LINEAR EFFECTS

The stencil is another routine that is standard in almost all Paintbox applications, as it offers a rapid and effective way of adding layers of images, and of adding colour effects to a controlled area of an image. The stencil creates much the same effect as the mask used by an airbrush artist, though of course in Paintbox any painting technique can be used to lay colour through a stencil. For example, in Sam Mandragona's record cover (on the facing page) a stencil was used to cut out the outline of the girl's face and then fill it with a single colour. By filling rather than airbrushing, the colour illuminance and density values in the underlying image could be preserved, to give a natural gradation of tone: airbrushing would have produced the risk of colour densities fluctuating.

A frequent use of stencil is to add highlights. Gary Hierons used a stencil cut from the mono lettering of the *Alles*

Alles Capito! logo for children's quiz programme (left).
Tyre advertisement by Sam Madragona (below, left).
'The Mirrors of the Soul' by Dale Coding (below, right).

Capito?! title logo firstly to add the rainbow colours (again using fill), and then airbrushed the white highlights to give an effect of depth. A stencil cut on Paintbox can be automatically reversed, to give an exact match, and it can also be rotated. In the tyre advertisement shown here, the outline of the road in the lower picture was adjusted, using stencil, to match the profile of the tyre design on the left.

This ability to rotate and move images, as well as the 'geometry set' for drawing lines, circles and ellipses, can be seen in Dale Coding's *Mirrors of the Soul*. Parts of the image were drawn using the Paintbox's toolkit for circles and straight lines, as well as stencil techniques and three-dimensional effects for copying, placing and adjusting sizes. The ability of Paintbox to move images around a three-dimensional axis is also seen in the true perspective of the floating square in the picture.

Millionaire Piglet and Driver Piglet (above), two advertisements for the Banca Bilboa Vizcaya created by Jurgen Krieger for Tandem DDB. A third image is facing, top right.

In graphics use, the smear command is particularly helpful for creating a sense of movement. In Mark Tatulli's drawing of *Frog Brick Face* a photo of a child's toy has been melded into a brick background, and the contours softened using smear, to give added impact to the image. In a series of bank advertisements, Jurgen Krieger used a piggy bank figure as the key character. By using smear on the motorized piggy bank's scarf, or on the money it is counting he suggests

(Centre) Sofia Alonso
used three photographs
by Genis Munoz in the fish
image produced for
clients Gobierno Vasco.
Mark Tatulli's Frog Brick
Face was created for a
children's television
programme (left).

rapid motion, making a double animated pun
out of the subject.

Another way to suggest movement is,
paradoxically, to stop it. The perceptual
conventions of the 'freeze frame' are well
established, so a third image in the piggy
bank series, with the drops from a watering
can frozen in mid-splash is read by the
viewer as an image in movement. Another
artist at Grafi-Image, Sofia Alonso, creates
the same effect with the picture of a fish

leaping into a tank of water. The Paintbox's
ability to challenge our perceptions in this
way is one of its most exciting characteristics.

This Volkswagen Golf convertible was put through the four seasons by Reinhard Ottenlinger of Laserscan (above). Advertisement for Perrier by Wiz-Art (right). Jim van Motman of Souverein used the Mont St Michel as a background for this sinister image (facing, above).

These four seasons views of a convertible, made by Reinhard Ottenlinger, are taken from a single image (that of the car under snow) and manipulated in Graphic Paintbox to create a convincing set of alternatives. Both additional photography and freehand drawing were used. Just as the Paintbox can accept and handle direct input, so input from photographs, transparencies and video can also be grabbed onto the system. Lief Sorsensen's Perrier advert combines three images, bottle, girl and lion, and uses the Paintbox to create a unifying background. Jim van Motman's hardly fairytale *Hitch Hiker* is based on eight of his own transparencies, and on using the Paintbox to adjust the lighting and colour balance to create a harmonious whole. Creating a similar image in a photographic studio, or through conventional laboratory techniques, would be immensely costly and complex, and not permit the endless variation of the image while in process that Paintbox allows.

GRAPHICS ON IMAGES

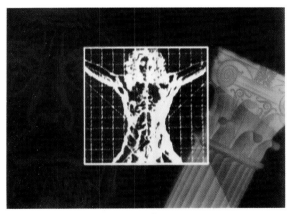

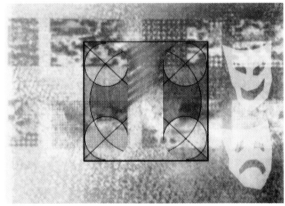

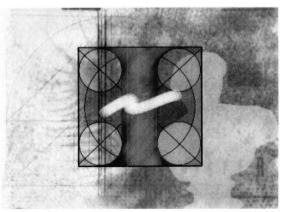

Four frames from a title sequence for the television arts programme Indicios, created by Zoom-TV, showing the progressive use of graphic elements against a changing background.

This advertisement for Kronenbourg beer was art directed by Jordi Almuni and worked on Paintbox by Ramon Ochando for Vincius Young and Rubicam in Barcelona. The elements used in the composition are shown.

Poster for the Nissan Pulsar, 1992.

Summit television news title for WB5TV, Boston.

Not only can photographic images be combined on Paintbox, but they can be mixed with other graphic images, for example with drawings or text. One of the commonest applications of Paintbox is in the television newsroom, where not only are graphics use to supplement news stories, but also in the convention of a 'running graphic' presented over the newsreader's shoulder and changing to illustrate changing stories. This device is now so commonplace that it is easy to forget the tight newsroom deadlines under which such creative work is often done. Michael Tiedeman's *Summit* shoulderboard

uses glass-cased lettering and mirror effects, perhaps to pun on the idea of a 'show-case' summit, while Catherine Krebs' *Housing Starts* places lettering over a set of mason's tools to lead into a graphic presentation, using numerals and an upward arrow.

Other combinations of graphics are between images and drawings: Jeff Mueller's promotional poster combines a transparency (with background removed) and a line drawing, while a poster from the Sohbi Corporation places a real car against a real sky and a drawn-in office building, conveniently highlighted with flash effects. Jordi Alumni combined a tennis ball, a study of water droplets and the Kronenbourg logo to suggest the best result of a thirsty game.

Crisp and mosaic effects were used to blend elements on this poster, art directed by Ken Butts for Franklin Laughlin and Constable (above).

Catherine Krebs of NBC News Graphics division created this full screen graphic sequence in November, 1992 (left).

Initial illustration and series of frames by Splash Computer Graphics for a children's television programme (top).
Frames from Paul Norris's P.O.S.H., wholly animated on Paintbox (middle).
Frames from a confectionery commercial by The Mill, London (below).

Video Paintbox systems also have animation capability, either from direct drawing, as in Paul Norris's *P.O.S.H.*, or by combining drawn images and live action, as with Tapestry's title sequence for a Welsh children's programme, or JSP's artful rendering of drawing into woman. The Mill's sweet commercial shows rather more dramatic manipulation of images in a three-dimensional animated space. Unlike traditional cell-animation, animation on Paintbox can be rendered more rapidly, and a range of other effects can be brought into use at the same time. Indeed with the

Paintbox the conventional divisions between media techniques become blurred and almost obsolete.

Animation into live action, from JSP Post's showreel (above).
Heidi Anderson created this electrical effect for a television title (right).

TEXTURES AND
COMBINED IMAGES

A series of different ways of treating the same image, through (clockwise from frame) colour fettle, overdrawing, pixelisation, changing backgrounds, and cut-and-tear, from Grafi-Image.

A series of images for the Bodyshop, created by Jon Turner and colleagues at Imagination, the London design and communications company. The images were used for showcards and window displays.

Bath

In conventional photography and printing, a textured effect can be given to an image through the use of special filters and screens, or through printing onto a textured surface. Providing visual texture on Paintbox by adding different backgrounds and effects, including using fettle to alter the colour balance, is shown in Toni Garretta's *Variations*.

In a series of posters and showcards for the Body Shop, Jon Turner wanted to create an overall canvas texture. The images were originally created on camera, by making-up the model to suggest one lighting solution, then lighting from a different angle to increase the contrast. The photographs were scanned into Paintbox, the textures and type added, and final adjustments to colour balance and detail made. One advantage of this approach was that the images could be presented on Paintbox, and adjustments (for example to product colours) carried out with the client until the last moment before output.

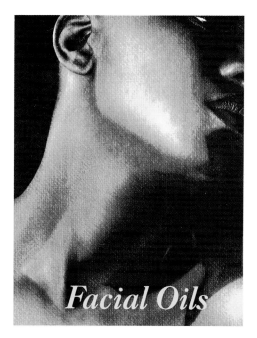

Facial Oils

Aromatherapy

Scentsationals

Combined images are especially useful in television work. Gary Hierons, at SAT1, Germany's independent satellite channel, used these images to provide links between successive programmes and to announce forthcoming items. The basic frame (top left) contained three framing elements, and video clips could be framed in each as well as traded between them, while, as the other frames show, the elements themselves could move. Shadow effects remained in track with the motion of the frame elements.

DISTORTION

Audrey van Aarsen's Twins 1 was created by mirror-imaging and distorting a colour image, Because the Paintbox maintains the same density of pixels even when an image is stretched, the colour values are not affected by the process. Lief Sorensen's multi-instrument *Orchestra* uses the Paintbox for colour matching and blending to build the single instrument from a range of elements.

'Twins 1' by Audrey van
Aarsen of Souverein

'Orchestra' by Lief
Sorenson of Wiz-Art

COLOUR EFFECTS

In the highly-coloured present day of television and advertising graphics, a simple monochrome statement may be particularly effective. Ironically, the age of Kennedy, bronzed out in R. Olsen's title card, saw the introduction of colour television in the USA: Rivka Bernstein's treatment of a contemporary photograph of Einstein may be more historically correct. Altered Images' use of a mono photograph as the basis for a glazing advert concentrates the viewer's attention on the product and its effect. The award-winning brochure from IQ Videographics deliberately uses a limited colour range of blue and red to make a striking statement. The image was comped together from three transparencies, then tint and wash functions were used to achieve the new colour balance. The fettle command on the Paintbox also allows the user to change the colour values overall, or through a series of colour pairings, to create strong colour distortions. By adjusting the colour curves, a progressive series of effects can be simulated and studied on screen. Luminance and contrast can also be changed. Colour fettling has been used on the background of the Grafi-Image *Magic of Colour*s poster, to take the rocks from brown and rust tones to blue and purple, and to transform the colour balance in parts of Go Asanuma's *Wright Brothers* calendar.

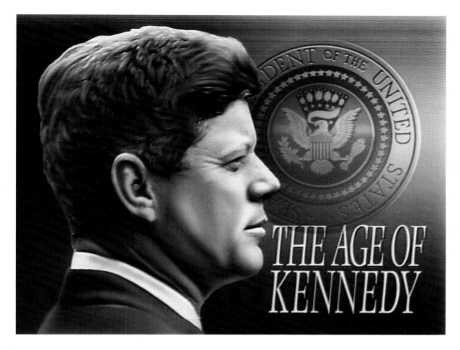

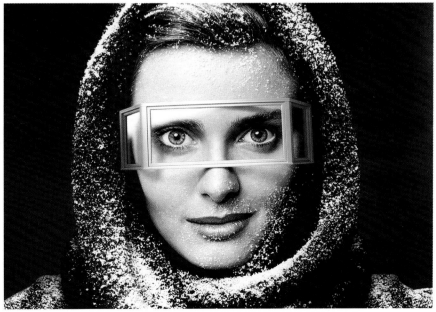

'The Age of Kennedy' by R. Olsen, art directed by John Bianco for NBC News Graphics in New York, director Ralph Famiglietta, Jnr. (top).

Advert for Weathershield Windows, for Hoffman, York and Compton, by Altered Images, from photography by Dennis Manarchy (middle).

Promo frame for '6/6' teenage magazine on Israel Educational Television, created by Rivka Bernstein (bottom).

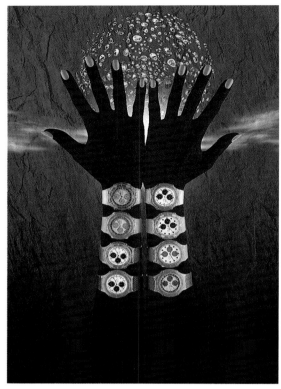

'Reaching Higher
Standards': an image from
a corporate brochure for
Rail Freight Distribution,
art directed by Michael
Denny,

designed by John
Bateson and Rachel
Dinnis, with Richard Baker
on Paintbox (left).
Roundel Design Group
were the clients.

Ramon Ochando of Grafi-
Image created this collage
for the company's own
publicity (seen above, with
two source
transparencies).

Three images from a
calendar 'Wright Brothers
– the Way to Kitty Hawk',
art directed and
photographed by Go
Asanuma, with Koichi
Kano as creative director
and Hidenori Kataoka as
Paintbox director, and
Aogu Kinosita and
Noriyuki Toyoda as
Paintbox artists. The client
was Ishikawajima-Harima
Heavy Industries Co.

LAYERING

Pittard Sullivan showcard (above).
Proposed opening sequence for television show 'First flights' by Videosmith (top right).
Two frames from a title sequence 'Outdoor photographer' by Paul Maras for Winner Communications (right).

The ability of Paintbox to handle different inputs of information non-hierarchically means that layers of images can be floated over one another, to create depths of meaning. Go Asanuma's *Wright Brothers* calendar also used this technique to good effect on a graphic Paintbox, and the technique has evident applications for Harriet and other television systems. Mark Tatulli's multi-layered showcard was for a proposed television show entitled *First Flights*, and Paula Mara's *Outdoor Photographer* sequence used multiple video images. Anna Maria Conte's *Cinema Estate* promo moved from overlays to collage to overlays so as to generate a multiplicity of images: a similar visual density is found in Pittard Sullivan's own showcard.

Video layering
exemplified by the
Cinema Estate trailer.

Sam Madragona, a
freelance Paintbox artist
in New York, captioned
these pictures 'examples
of retouching'. In fact, it
is virtually impossible to
say which is the first and
which the second state of
retouching.

CONCLUSION

Introducing the first BBC Design Awards, the design writer John Thackara spoke of modern image handling technology as ushering in a new definition of reality and realism as important as the discovery of perspective or the invention of photography. Few would doubt that in saying such things he had the Paintbox in mind. The ability of the Paintbox to amend, improve and transform images challenges traditional views of representation. William J. Mitchell, professor of architecture at M.I.T. has written on the nature and consequences of 'the displacement of photography', in *The Reconfigured Eye*, MIT Press, 1992, and other recent books on Virtual Reality and Cyberspace have posed questions on the current status of the representation of reality. This is an important issue, and one that is not going to go away once the hubbub over a new technology declines.

The generally accepted notion of the representational truth of the photograph as a 'mechanical analogue of reality' in Barthes's terms is wholly undermined by the ability of the Paintbox to create new images and manipulate old ones into new images with the same apparent values of consistency and redundancy as photographs. When we look at a photograph, we use, even if subconsciously, our knowledge of perspective to evaluate whether the photograph is consistent with perceived reality: the Paintbox image mirrors these perceptual shortcuts. Similarly, photographs are rich in informational content, much of which is redundant to the message of the photograph, but which reinforces our definition of the image as a photograph (as compared to a line drawing, for example). Paintboxed images achieve the same density of content (compared to computer-generated images, where the density is not always high enough to be wholly convincing.) Take the two still lives by Sam Mandragona. One is the original photograph, one is the imaged subtly changed on Paintbox (the apple has changed position, as has the bow of the violin). There

is no way of telling which image is which, either from its printed form or from the transparencies: they contain equally convincing levels of information, presented in 'realistic' ways. Indeed, since the two images I received were unlabelled, I do not even know which one is the original!

In the photograph, as Barthes has pointed out, the analogon is mediated by the choices and attitudes of the photographer, the publisher of the photograph and the reader. The photograph contains an analogous denoted message, the 'content' of the image, and a culturally determined connoted message, the 'interpretation' of the image. Barthes was particularly concerned with the reading of newspaper photography, and in the total statement made by both photograph and caption. In his view, an important part of the connoted message was that a photograph was a record of an actual event, that it made the statement 'the photographer was there: the action in the image took place.' This assumption of the veracity of photographs is widespread, and is found in the old cliche that the camera cannot lie.

This part of the message, this instant acceptance that reality is represented in an image, no longer holds with a Paintboxed image. Indeed, many Paintboxed images deliberately make an impossibility of the statement 'this took place,' by the way the image is constructed. But by extension, the existence of Paintbox technology vitiates the claim of realism of all subsequent photography, for from the final reproduced image itself there is no way of telling whether a once-photographed image has been handled by a Paintbox or not. This does not mean that the connoted 'content' of the image disappears, it merely requires the viewer or reader to bring other faculties of judgment to bear on the image to understand it.

The most widespread use of Paintboxing is in news reporting, where images are created to help the viewer to relate more rapidly to complex contemporary issues, or in television titling, which is simple

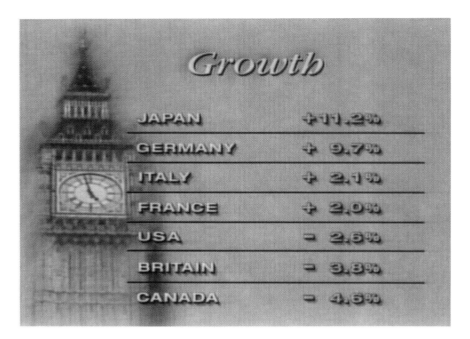

Growth

JAPAN	+ 11.2%
GERMANY	+ 9.7%
ITALY	+ 2.1%
FRANCE	+ 2.0%
USA	− 2.6%
BRITAIN	− 3.8%
CANADA	− 4.6%

Aida Milbergs of NBC News Graphics in Washington D.C. produced these video visuals for the July 1991 economic summit. Does the deliberate evocation of traditional portraiture affect our perception of the news...

entertainment. Nevertheless, there are some who would see sinister or unwelcome aspects to the development of a technology that tinkers with representation, fearing that digital imaging could be used to produce fraudulent proofs or to re-write historical truth. This attitude ignores the fact that 'faked' photographs – from the cardboard butterfly on Walt Whitman's photographic self-portrait to Stalinist editings of Lenin haranguing the masses without Trotsky in attendance – have been around from the beginning of photography. In the final analysis, every photograph only tells a partial truth, either through the selection of viewpoint and the cropping of the image, or more subtly through the choice of depth of focus, lens length and shutter speed, as well as through the conversion of the endless colours of the real world into either monochrome or the three tint gels of colour film. The received idea of photographic 'truth' is therefore itself an approximation of reality, and was so before Paintbox. On the positive side, digital image handling has increased immensely the scientific knowledge available from images taken by exploration satellites such as Voyager, and the application of digital imaging in medicine and research has had enormous benefits, in presenting logical constructs of literally invisible phenomena.

A photograph is only ever a mediated representation of reality, a fact which our familiarity with photography tends to blur. What in fact digital imaging has done is to put into sharper contrast those aspects of photography itself which did not square with the received view of photography as representing reality in a solely mechanical way. Having thus made a fiction of photography, digital technology has gone on to extend the range of fictions, and devise new and more challengingly ambiguous relations with reality. Just as the invention of photography a century and a half ago did not provoke the death of painting, rather a kind of resurrection, so digital imaging is providing a new challenge to photography, and in a wider sense a challenge to our understanding of reality.

Another distinction between photography and digital imaging is more subtle. A camera produces a single, definable object, a photographic negative. Leaving aside the question of how the negative may be treated by cropping or processing to create further images, the photographic negative can be seen as a fixed element, an original keystone. Thus the negative normally remains in the ownership of the photographer, who can control the number and the quality of the prints taken from it. The negative is also fixed in time: at one point it commences to exist. The Paintbox image also has a start point in time, but is not subject to closure in the same way. A Paintboxed image can be subjected to endless transformation: it is never fixed. Unlike the analogue image produced by a photographic camera, a Paintbox image is only a stream of digital information. The stream can be endlessly changed into new patterns, can be output in different ways, and can be taken over and adapted by others. The material for the main section of this book came in on six different video formats, as 35mm and full scale transparencies, as magneto-optical disks, as colour prints, as video prints, as printed matter. Each was a valid format for presenting a Paintboxed work: none was *the* sole valid format. One contributor, for example, sent in several versions of the same piece as it evolved. As William Mitchell points out, the term 'digital camera' often applied to recording devices is a misnomer, though an understandable one: a camera makes a fixed, analogue record, which is precisely what a digital camera does not do.

A creative work that does not have a fixed version raises immediate problems of intellectual property, copyright and control. These problems are complex ones, and it is in the interests of the whole creative community that the practical questions they pose be solved. But beyond such legal considerations, the fluid nature of Paintboxed work, its endless transmutability, also sets it apart from other creative enterprise. The distinction between finished work and work in progress is wholly blurred, as is the definition of an 'original state'. Of course, this is a theoretical problem in trying to define the nature of Paintboxing, not a problem that frequently arises in Paintbox work as such. (Rather, it occurs as a benefit. Several designers have told me how useful it is to make presentations on Paintbox so that changes requested by clients can be incorporated rapidly, and before output costs are incurred.) This problem touches what could be termed the post-Modern aspect of Paintbox.

Post-Modernism is a term barely fifteen years old, but in some respects it has not worn well. In architecture (where the term originated) it has become popularly assimilated to flabby decoration applied to dull buildings, for example. But no other term describes so aptly the parallel and

...or are we better off with visual puns (as in Catherine Krebs' NBC title on anti-sniper training for children) or with deliberately complex imagery, as in Framestore's title sequence for a reconstruction of the Cuban missile crisis (above)?

41

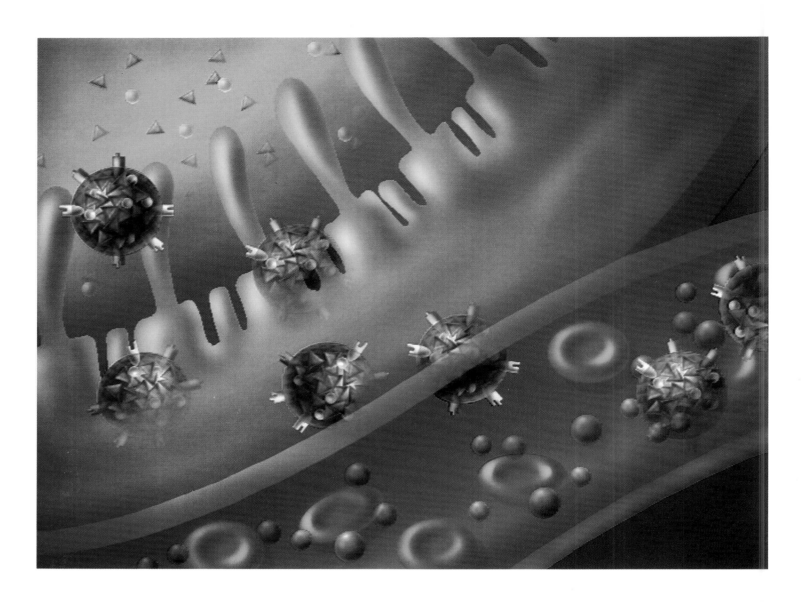

Paintbox in the service of science and information: the upper illustration shows the absorption of lipoproteins into intestinal capillaries, produced by Therese Trebaol for Lifetime Medical Television, and the lower an info graphic produced by Mary Webb for the Central Intelligence Agency.

shared developments in various aspects of the arts and sciences concerned with re-evaluating traditional rules and codes in a freer spirit. The post-Modern approach is multiple, open-ended, ambiguous, collaged, self-aware. In opposition to the classical rules of Modernism and earlier credos, it proposes metaphor, humour and mixture. It accepts that hierarchies are over and certainties are dead, and that semiotics, not functions, are the models for discourse. In the physical sciences this new approach dovetails with chaos theory as well as with new techniques in sociology. In the humanities it informs literary criticism, and adds to our understanding of contemporary art. The Paintbox, with its open-ended, unsystematic approach to the interface with the user, with its potential to manipulate and extend imagery, and with its allographic creative potential, seems to me the very model of the post-Modern machine. The use of Paintboxes in contexts where the post-Modern effect is most visible – television, advertising and design – only serves to heighten this role. Previously machines were structured: they performed set tasks within defined rules and limits: they required trained operators and a disciplined approach. Contemporary machines have choice and multiplicity thought into them. This process goes beyond the cliche of user-friendly, to a new, post-Modern definition of the role of the machine, and the Quantel Paintbox stands at the apex of this new definition.

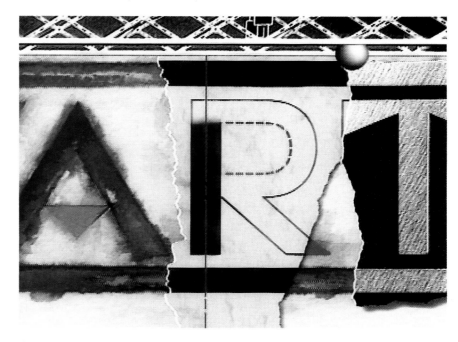

Or perhaps the Paintbox is only art. Television title by the Framestore, Paintbox artist Mike McGee.

Information
Title by Avenue Edit.

THE BEST ELECTRONIC IMAGES

The images on the following pages were selected from materials submitted following a general invitation to all Quantel Paintbox operators worldwide. No invitations for specific images were made, and, provided images had been handled in Paintbox in some way, all were considered for inclusion. The choice highlighted the ephemeral nature of much Paintboxed material: I was often aware that what I was seeing was private work, or work from a personal portfolio; often, I suspect, because other work was no longer available.

In making the selection, I tried to let the community of Paintbox artists speak for itself, by paying attention to the use that was to be made of the original material: after all, someone asked to devise a news graphic with less than half a day's notice is in a different position from an independent artist with potentially unlimited time, or from someone with an advertising client to satisfy. So the selection deliberately tries to reflect all the different applications Paintboxes are put to work on, rather than establishing a fixed canon of what constitutes 'good work'. For example, I'm very much aware that the printed reproduction quality of some video images may never be as high as of graphic ones, and equally that the fluid and changing nature of video images can never be properly treated in print. The order of work is only roughly alphabetical: for full details see the index.

The collaborative nature of work on Paintbox, particularly in commercial work, was very clear, and those submitting work were asked to cite their co-workers, clients or partners, as they wished. In labelling work either to individuals or to enterprises I have tried to respect the spirit of this. What I hope the user of this book will share is the enjoyment I got from looking at so many images: I'm only sorry I didn't have twice as many pages to fill!

Audrey van Aarssen

Audrey van Aarssen is a Paintbox artist with Souverein at Weesp in the Netherlands. Born in Melbourne, Australia in 1965, she worked in lithography for two years before moving to Paintbox: she sees the potential of the machine for making fashion-related images more noticeable and visible.

Orchid Dream

Original artwork created by Audrey van Aarssen from two transparencies, 1992: photography by Miriam Jeurissen, make-up by Nicky Knippenberg, with Sabina Eblingkoning as model.

Twins Two

Original artwork created by Audrey van Aarssen from a single transparency, 1991: photography by Miriam Jeurissen, make-up by Nicky Knippenberg, with Katalina Brandsma as model.

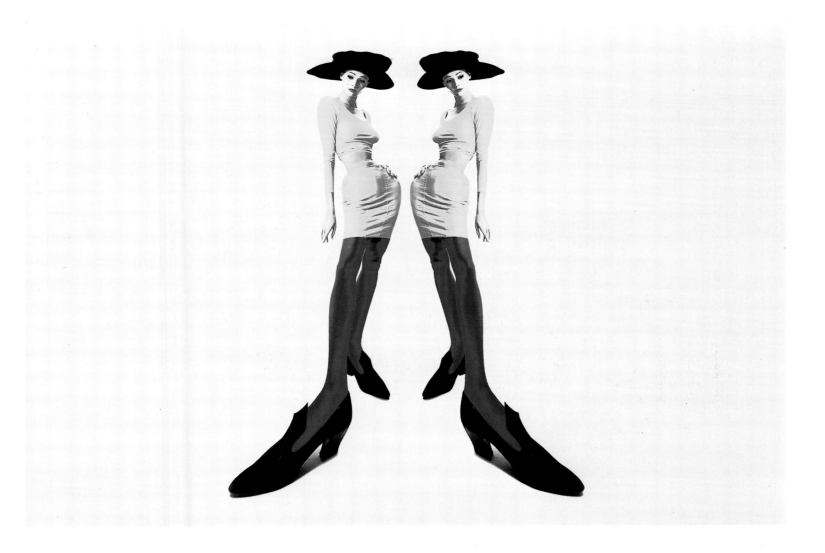

Ad Libitum Trannys

This company, in Crows Nest, New South Wales, Australia, are Graphic Paintbox specialists.

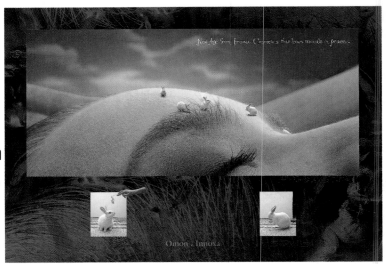

Imoxa

This cosmetics advertisement, for Omon, was art directed by Malcolm Pointon and designed by Simon Whiteley.

Orthoxicol

Designed by Simon Whiteley and art directed by Chris Bull, this image featured on a point of sale card commissioned by Sudler and Hennessey.

Self promotion

This image was designed by Simon Whiteley for Ad-Lib's corporate use.

Altered Images

Jeff and Brent Mueller are the Paintbox artists at Altered Images Inc in Milwaukee, USA, providing design and consultancy services to a range of clients, as varied as those mixed into their promotional showcard.

Brochure Cover

Created for A.O. Smith Inc, though Communicor, and art directed by Mark Fossen, this image combines scanned industrial elements with a rich and sombre colour background.

Trek Bike Catalogue Cover

A deceptively simple image composed for Frankenberry, Laughlin and Constable, and art directed by Mark Koerner.

Miller Draft

Designed by Brandon Adams for BZIGN, this poster was published in 1992.

Altered Images Promo

Art directed by John Grieder of Cramer-Krasselt, this 1992 showcard uses a total of eleven transparencies to create a modern image of corporate man.

50

Aogu Kinoshita

This series of ten 'Works' was created on the
graphic Paintbox facilities at Sohbi
Corporation, Tokyo, by Aogu Kinoshita.
Later exhibited, the pieces won a bronze
award in the 1992 JACA exhibition.

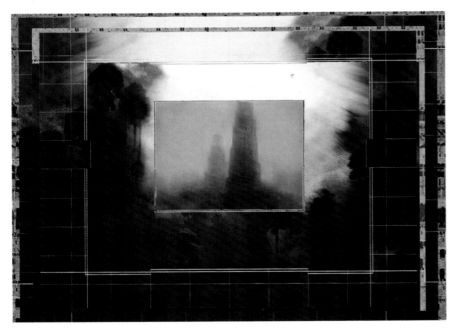

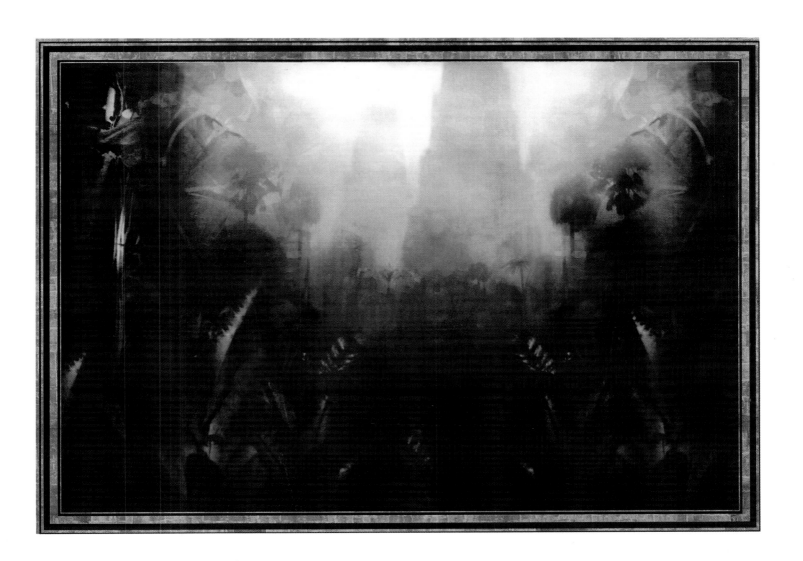

Avenue Edit

The Chicago company Avenue Edit provides Paintbox services for television commercials, programme titles and for pop videos.

Watering Can

This TV commercial for Volkswagen was made in 1991 for DDB Needham Inc, and produced by Mary Kondrat with Doug Wood as art director. As animated water falls on the back of a sedan, it grows greenly into an estate car. The Paintbox artists were Heidi Anderson and Mark Ward, and the commercial won a 1992 Telly Award.

Dance

Designed and art directed by Michelle Sundry, this music video for Reid Brody took step-framed images of dancers and, after editing and distorting them on Paintbox restrung them into a fluid, continuous sequence.

55

Bruce Eric Brauer

Bruce Eric Brauer, now a freelance Paintbox artist, has worked with the team of Paintbox artists working with the News Graphics division of NBC in New York.

Title shot

A reworking of a familiar American icon to provide a header for a personal demo reel.

Angel in the Sky

Designed for NBC Network News Graphics, director Ralph Famiglietta Jnr., the image of the girl was drawn in pencil, scanned in and developed on the Paintbox.

Kevin J. Barr

Kevin Barr is a Paintbox artist living in Lansdowne, Philadelphia. He works for Palette Studios in Philadelphia, a Graphic Paintbox facility. The works shown here are his original artworks.

White Collar Worker

Words and image by
Kevin Barr, 1992

The Great Seal

Image by Kevin Barr, with latin text from the US dollar bill, 1992

Cowfolk

Words and image by
Kevin Barr, 1992

At a liquid sunset
silently breathing
white noise,
a sacred cow drops in

to observe
a glowing triptych
of Hank, Ethel and Harriet
sinking into time.

Bruce Brouwn

Bruce Brouwn works as a Paintbox artist with Souverein in Weesp. He was one of the first Paintbox artists at Souverein, and is one of the most experienced.

Portrait

This image uses the old trick of anamorphic projection, whereby an image will only be readable in a columnar mirror placed on the image. Conceived and designed by Bruce Brouwn.

Self-Portrait

Commissioned as a cover for Focus magazine, this unflattering image was photographed by Bieneke Koedijk and art directed and designed by Bruce Brouwn.

Egg Observation

Designed by Bruce
Brouwn from an original
photograph by Leen
Thysse.

British Sky Broadcasting

This London-based satellite television company uses in-house Paintbox and Harriet facilities for titles and on-screen graphics.

The Movie Channel

This twelve second monthly promo, designed by Mark Hyde, combines Paintbox and Abekas work and live action.

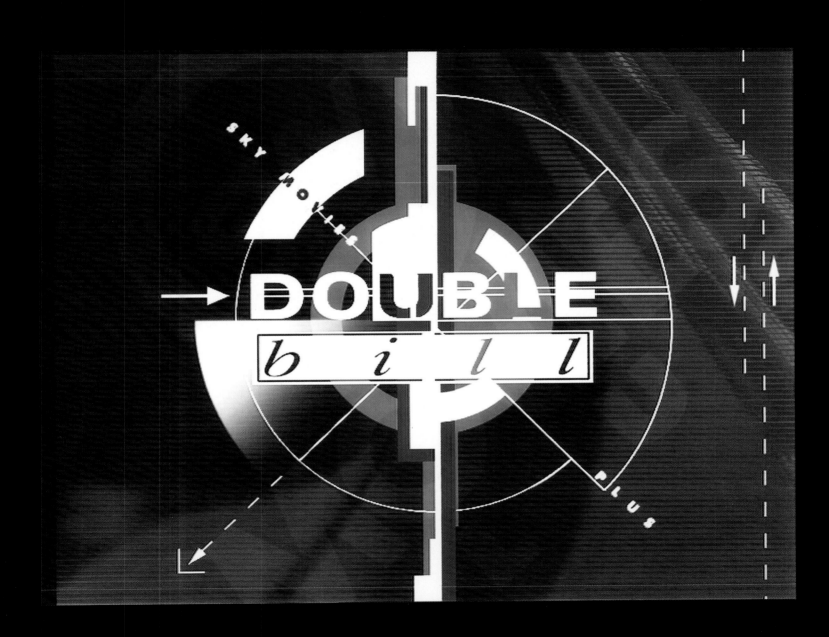

Sky Movies Plus

An eight second sequence
as an opening feature for a
double programme,
designed by Mark Hyde.

Centro Digital Pictures

Centro Digital offer Paintbox agency services to the Hong Kong and South East Asian design community. Recruiting Paintbox artists in Hong Kong and from as far afield as London, New York and Toronto, the company offers both video and graphic facilities.

Spotted Dog

Art directed by Thomas Lim for clients Backer, Spielvogel Bates Ltd in Hong Kong, this advertisement for Shell is based on two transparencies. The Paintbox artist was Dee Dee Donnelly

Mitsukoshi

This advertisement for Asatsu International Ltd involved scanning in three transparencies and then handling the floating leaves in perspective to generate the desired effect, as well as colour correction. The Paintbox artists were Dale Coding and Dee Dee Donnelly.

Elena Chiesa

In 1991 Elena Chiesa and Todd Ruff's Green Movie won first prize for 2-D animation at PIXELINA in Monte Carlo. She works as an independent Paintbox artist in Milan, having trained in Rome, Genoa and Milan in animation. Work for IBM has also won her a first prize at Audiovidex, 1987.

Green Movie

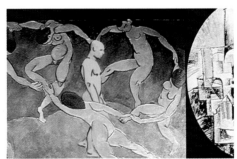

The Nine Lives of Menelao

Made as a series of still images, Elena Chiesa describes the purpose of this work simply as 'fun'.

Green Movie

A two minute promotional digital movie for the Green Movie Post Production Studio. Art directed, written and designed by Todd Ruff and Elena Chiesa, it shows a single figure striding out of Grunewald's Isenheim altarpiece and through a series of encounters with famous paintings from Giorgione to van Gogh and beyond.

Eric Coignoux

Eric Coignoux is a freelance Paintbox artist working in Paris. His short promotional animation Money was made for MTV entirely on Paintbox, using the facilities at Mikros-Image in Paris.

Anna Conte

Based in Milan, and with three year's Paint-box experience, the designer Anna Conte has won freelance commissions from Philips for advertising and from other companies for corporate design work. She has a particular liking for British graphic design: 'always up to date and at the same time full of ancient memories'.

Happy Man

Independent graphic by Anna Conte, based on a photograph and drawing of the British Member of Parliament Paul Boateng.

Sad Man

Independent graphic by
Anna Conte, designed and
created entirely on
Paintbox.

English & Pockett

Bob English and Darell Pockett's London-based agency is hardly ten years old, but has already won awards for its television work with Paintbox.

ITV Sport
A programme title for the ITV association, designed by Simon Martin.

01 for London
Designed by Harry Darrington for Mentom films.

Anglia

Promotional item for the
commercial TV station
Anglia, designed by
Darrell Pockett.

Kristian Esser

Kristian Esser's letterhead shows an artist's easel with a cord and electric plug on the end. It neatly encapsulates his role as an electronic illustrator. Esser works in Amsterdam, using the Paintbox facilities at Souverein in Weesp. His work as a Paintbox artist has been shown at the Canon Gallery and the Rijksmuseum. All these images are independent pieces from his own illustrations.

Absolut Esser

This illustration was exhibited at the Stedjelik Museum in May 1993.

Twins

Time

Independent work directed
and designed by Kristian
Esser, using his own
illustrations and the
Paintbox facilities at
Souverein.

Christine Finn

Christine Finn is a graphic designer who uses
Paintbox in her work as senior designer at
WCVB TV5 in Boston. She has won
numerous awards for her work.

Station identity for WCVB TV

Programme logos

Five Turns Twenty

Two draft versions and
the final version of a title
card for the twentieth
anniversary of the station
in 1992.

Framestore

Established specialists in Paintbox services for broadcasting, the Framestore in London's Covent Garden uses rostrum and live action effects in combination with Paintbox.

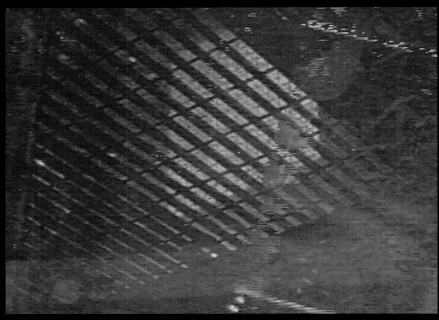

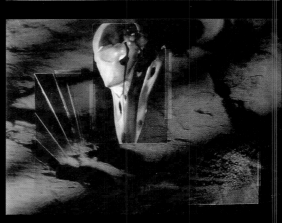

Terror Town
Part of a sequence for the BBC's Opera New Year, designed by J.G. Hills.

Stab in the Dark
This title sequence for Channel 4 was designed by Chris Mortimer.

Lucifer
J.G. Hills designed this image, using a live actor, for Channel 4.

Underbelly
Designed for a Channel 4 series.

The Sorceress
Designed by J. G. Hills for
Channel 4, the chariot and
actress are real.

Francesco Frongia

Francesco Frongia is an independent Paintbox artist working in Milan, using the facilities at Pool Video Centre. He specializes in work for television, such as the Tra Poco title sequence for a comedy programme shown here.

GRAFX Creative Imaging

The three creative partners in Grafx (a division of Tukaiz Innovative Prepress) based in Franklin Park, Illinois, are Daniel M. Bennett, Jose Campos and Scott Harding. They firmly believe that the creative use of the Graphic Paintbox for non-commercial subjects, such as those illustrated here, provides an additional way of encouraging their commercial clients to understand the potential of the machine and the services they offer.

Jose Campos
Kabuki

This haunting image was created directly onto the Paintbox using airbrush mode, without pre-scanned images.

Jose Campos
Marble You Say?

This combination of airbrushed image and marble texture was embossed in colour, then passed through an Apple Mac system to define the contours of the head. It was returned to the Paintbox to finish the details of the face and shadows.

Dan Bennett
Wet Bricks

A layered image of mortar, water and brickwork derived from three photographs, smear brushwork and scanned stencil.

Scott Harding
Treefrog

Texture stencils were used to enhance the details of original artwork in this 1991 illustration.

Jose Campos
Red E or Not

This Ernst-like image was built up from a background scanned image with airbrush overlay to create the figure.

Dan Bennett
Self-Portrait

Subtitled 'I'm not that homely', this image is truly interactive: 'I placed my face on the JX-600 scanner for the duration to get the unflattering RGB image and illustrated the rest.'

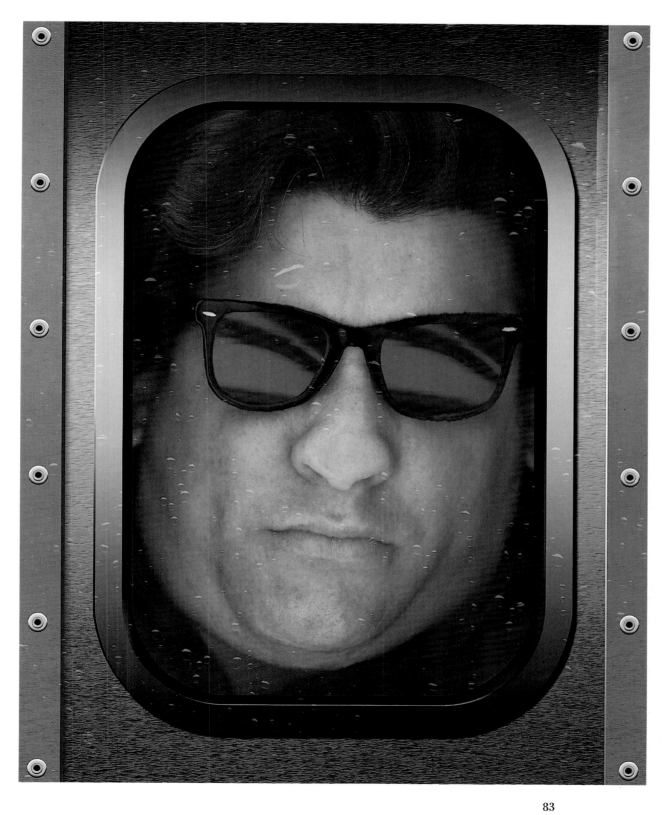

Grafi-Image

The Barcelona-based Grafi-Image provides design and agency services for Paintbox graphics to advertising and design. It was the first company to be set up in Spain offering Paintbox services.

Nissan

The "emboss" technique was used to set the Nissan logo in stone for this promotional brochure, art directed by Nuria Vilaseca for Denada Communicacion, SA, Barcelona.

Paraiso

This advertising image for perfume was produced for McCann Erickson Barcelona, and art directed by Vicky Ribalte from photography by Leandro Escofet and Stefano Morini. It was produced for a June 1992 campaign.

Appel Kas

Three photographs by Daniel Font were melded into this cheerful advert, art directed by Juan Romero for the Barcelona office of Saatchi & Saatchi. It was used for the launch of Appel Kas in Spain.

Stone Woman/ Landscape with Cup

Artists Toni Garreta and David Texidor combined a range of different images and techniques to create these two sequential images for Grafi-Image's own publicity. A total of twenty-four images were scanned and retouched to create these images, on which colour values were then balanced and shadows added.

April Grieman

The leading figure in New Wave West Coast graphics, April Grieman has worked closely with digital imagery, as well as moving into interior and furniture design.

Workspace

Designed as a poster for the Moscone Center in San Francisco, this poster was created on Paintbox with Bob Engelsiepen of View Studio, with additional design on Apple Macintosh.

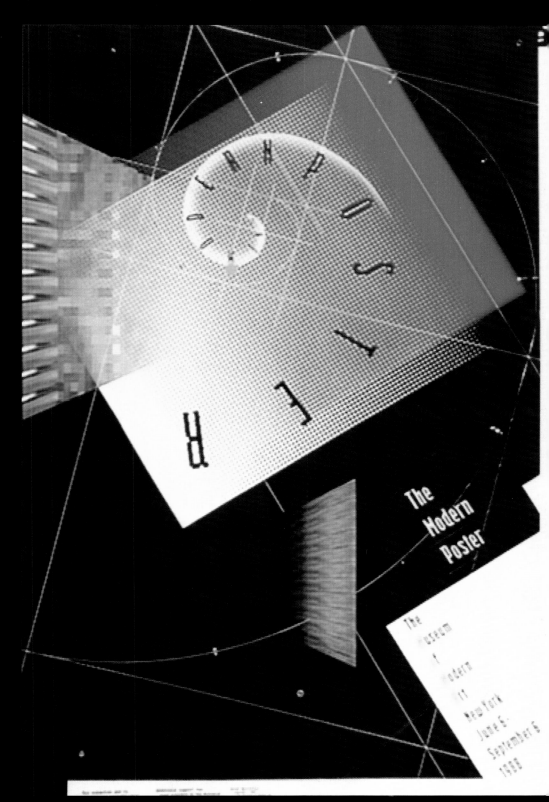

The Modern Poster

Created for the Museum of Modern Art, New York, this poster was produced on Paintbox and Apple Macintosh with Bob Engelsiepen of View Studio.

The Modern Poster

The Museum of Modern Art, New York June 6, September 6 1988

IBM

The Skill Dynamics Media Centre (Skill Dynamics is an IBM company) at Marietta, Georgia, USA, makes extensive use of Paintbox systems for preparing information and training material on video for IBM's use.

Computer based training

This training video was art directed and designed by Anita Critz, with Andy Johnson as writer and Beth Goodwin as producer. The Paintbox was not only used to create graphic stills but also to create the storyboard for client approval.

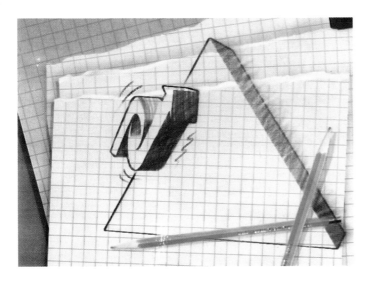

Vision to Reality

The video was produced in January 1992 as part of the Motivation programme of IBM's US education service. These graphics were art directed and designed by Anita Critz, with writer Amy Wiesleman.

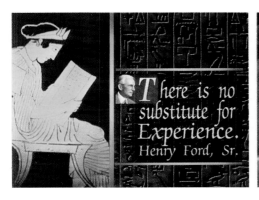

There is no substitute for Experience.
Henry Ford, Sr.

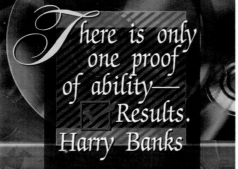

There is only one proof of ability— Results.
Harry Banks

LEARN

IQ Videographics

Opened in 1986 as the first design company
using Graphic Paintbox, IQ Videographics
have provided design, production and
consultancy services for a wide range of
clients, from the Ford Motor Company to the
English National Opera, and Novell
Computers to the Royal Mail.

In-House Brochure

Art directed and designed
by Richard Baker and
Mark Bullen, with texts by
Lyn Cushing, typography
by Richard Wolfstrome
and photography by Mark
Bullen, and produced as
an 710 x 185 flyer.

CLIENT: TDK
DESIGN: Siobhan Keaney
SUBJECT: Poster

CLIENT: Sire Records
DESIGN: Stylo Rouge
SUBJECT: Danielle Dax
album sleeve

CLIENT: Metropolis 88
DESIGN: Metropolis 88
SUBJECT: Self promotion

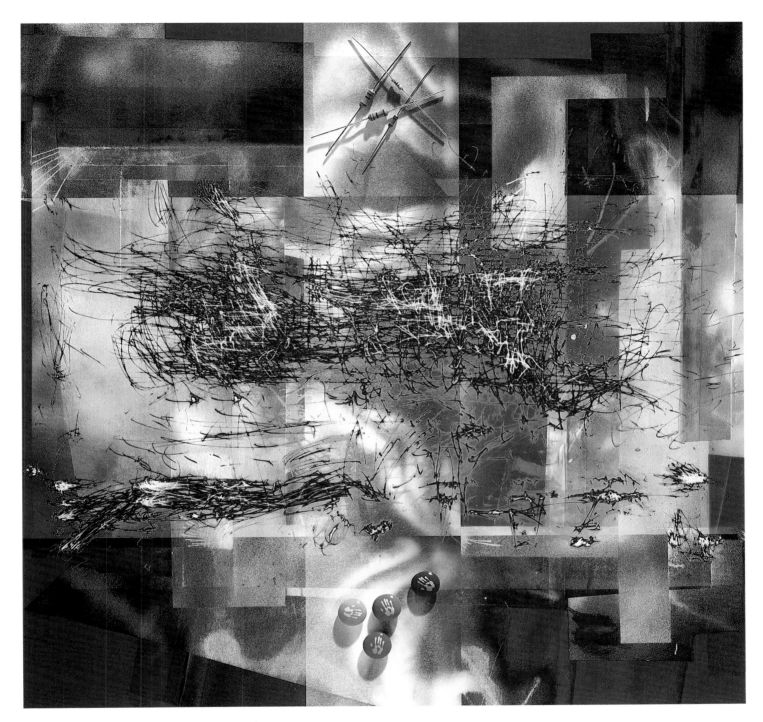

Scribbles

Produced as in-house advertising for the company, this graphic was designed by Mark Bullen using high-definition video images and tracings of actual hand movements during a real job. Extensive stencils and complex colour re-workings created the final version.

JSP Post

JSP Post is a post-production company producing high-end television commercials for the whole South-East Asia region. These shots are from the header to a promotional showreel designed by Caroline Liew, head of the Paintbox department.

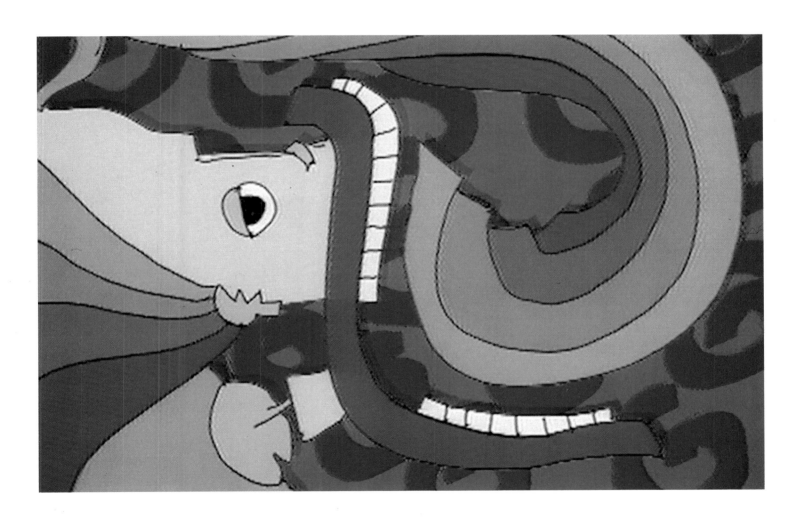

Water Kerner

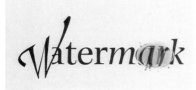

James Dean: The Image and the Man

A 10 second video sequence developed for an open exhibition, based on the American hero James Dean. Colour camerawork, direct manipulation and images of paper towels were used.

Water Kerner runs her own design agency, Watermark, in Los Angeles, California. Previous work for Tape House Digital in New York as digital effects designer creating material for television includes the MTV ident shown here. The 1991 showreel on James Dean was for Watermark.

Joy Ride

15 second network ID video, 1992, designed and directed by Water Kerner and produced/co-directed by Mindi Lipschultz at Tape House.

In-House Pro-Motion

This 10 second video to
promote Tape House Digital
was art directed and
designed by Water Kerner
in 1991. Stills from it were
also used for labelling.

Karin Spyker

Born in 1966 in the Netherlands, Karin Spyker trained as a textile-design teacher and artist before turning to graphic work. She is now a Paintbox artist working with Souverein at Weesp in Holland.

Girlfriends

Independent work designed by Karin Spyker from a small-format transparency, via stencilling and colour alteration, 1992.

Woman with Hat

Independent work designed by Karin Spyker from a black and white drawing, 'giving the picture a new, cheerful dimension' as she says.

Laserscan ArtBox Studio

This Dusseldorf-based company specializes in Graphic Paintbox work.

Samson and the Circus

One of a series of poster images for Samson tobacco, for DMB&B Imparc, designed by Reinhard Ottenlinger, art directed by Knievels. This one uses a photograph from the Circus Roncalli.

Comic

Designed and drawn by Reinhard Ottenlinger from an original photograph.

Marlene

An airbrush illustration created by Reinhard Ottenlinger, 1990.

M² Design

M² Design was started by Michael Marlow and Micha Riss in New York in 1990. Originally specializing in video work, they now also handle graphic commissions.

Breaking the Mold

Designed as a photo mural for a 1992 Merrill Lynch conference, with Graphic Paintbox work by Tito Saubidet.

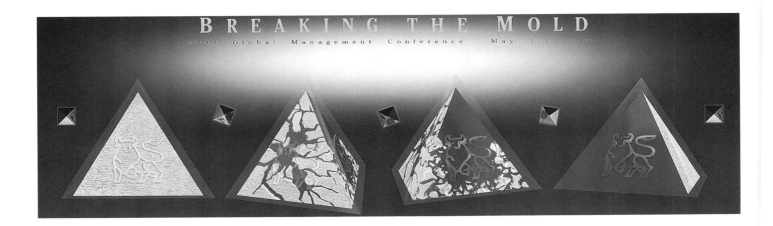

NFL

TV promotion for CBS Sports, using live action over animated backgrounds. M² also created a new ident for CBS Sports.

All Stars

TV promotion for the 1992 baseball season.

Dolphins Whales & Us

Created as an opening
sequence for a CBS
documentary: 30 hours of
film were analyzed to
create the 30 second
sequence on Harry.

Kim Mannes-Abbott

A first generation Paintbox artist, Kim Mannes-Abbott exhibited images derived from Paintbox studies at her diploma show, and has since worked in America, Japan and Europe almost exclusively with electronic graphics for video and print. She now lives in Holland, working as a designer with Souverein, and producing her own independent artworks, as well as developing commissions for clients.

New York Trilogy

Independent work designed and directed by Kim Mannes-Abbott, 1991, using two 35mm transparencies shot by Hans Petersen, and composed on the Paintbox facilities at Souverein. The image and title reflect Paul Auster's *New York Trilogy*.

Angels in America

Independent work designed and directed by Kim Mannes-Abbott, 1991, using three 35mm transparencies shot by Miriam Jeurissen. The image appeared in XYZ Direction magazine in 1992.

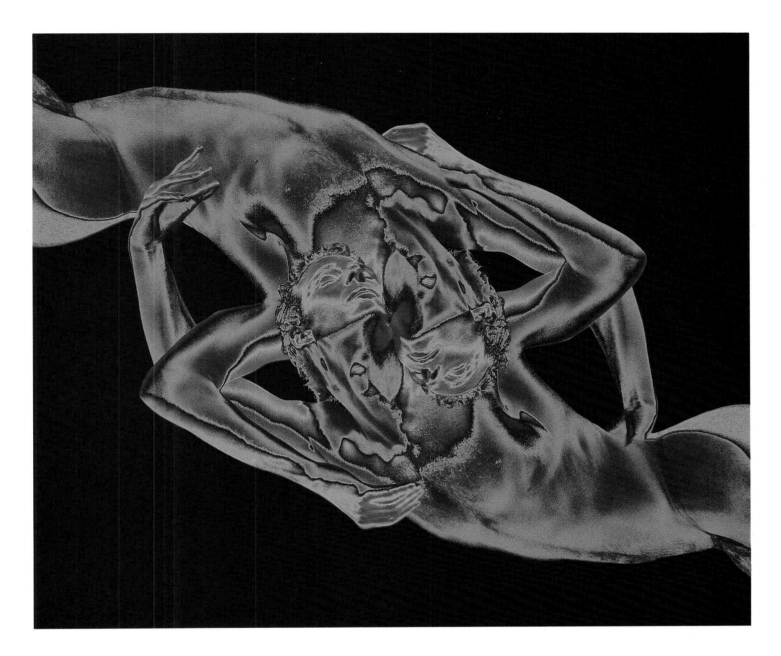

Moon Palace

Independent work
designed and directed by
Kim Mannes-Abbott, 1992
using transparencies shot
by Hans Petersen. The
image and title reflect Paul
Auster's *Moon Palace*.

Blue Steel

Independent work
designed and directed by
Kim Mannes-Abbott,
1992, photography by
Hans Petersen.

The Mill

Based in London, The Mill specialises in video Paintbox services for advertising agencies and television.

Rolo 'Hare'

This advert, animated by Klactoveesedstene, was created on Harry by Owen Hurley, for the J. Walter Thompson agency.

Cadbury's Boost 'Stagecoach'

The agency was Bartle
Bogle Hegarty, and work
on Harry was done by
Tom Sparks.

Kodacolour 'Soldier'

Created on Harry by Tom
Sparks for the agency
Young and Rubicam.

Weetabix 'Trojan Horse'

Tom Sparks produced this
job on Harry for Lowe
Howard-Spink.

Halifax 'House'

A promotion for a Building
Society, created on Harry
by Owen Hurley for BSB
Dorland

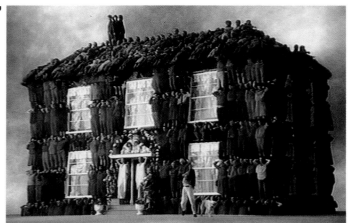

Pittard Sullivan Fitzgerald

Pittard Sullivan Fitzgerald is a Hollywood-based
Paintbox agency, the result of a merger between
Pittard Sullivan Design, well known for
television titles, and Wayne Fitzgerald, who
produce film titles.

Cher at the Mirage

Promotion created for
CBS.

Newsview

This news title was
created for Vu Produc-
tions by designer Flavio
Kampah and art director
Ed Sullivan.

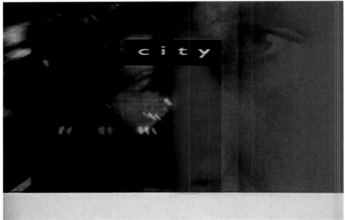

Angel City

Designed for Hearst
Entertainment by Jeff
Boortz, art directed by Ed
Sullivan.

E! Planet Hollywood

TV title designed by
Flavio Kampah and
directed by Billy Pittard
for E! Entertainment
Television

Sohbi Corporation

The Sohbi Corporation in Tokyo, Japan, is involved in providing both Graphic Paintbox services to design agencies and in direct creative work.

Iyugatsu

Original artwork created and designed by Hiroshi Saito.

Sea, Green, Sahara

A series of three posters for FM Japan, designed by Tadatoshi Kobayashi, art direction by Masahisa Nakamura created on Graphic Paintbox by Aogu Kinosita, directed by Hidenori Kataoka.

Mercedes Poster

The complex effects of front wing damage were created entirely on screen from a single colour transparency.

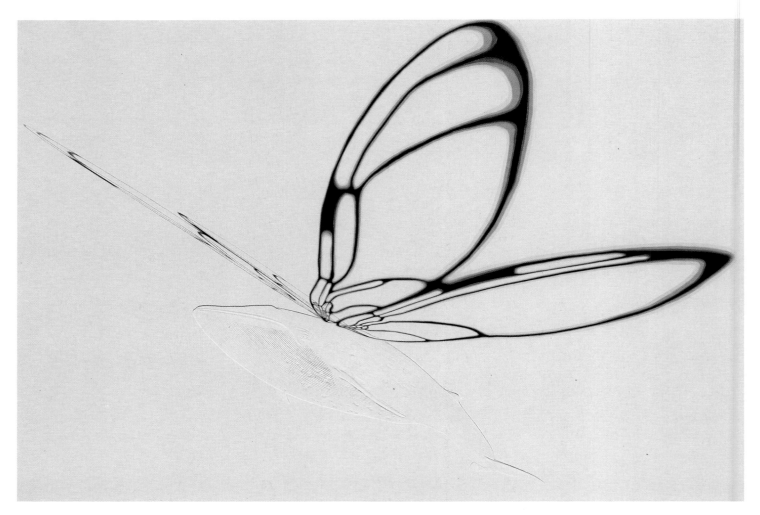

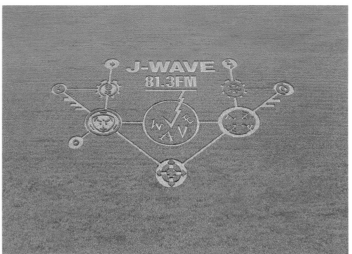

Souverein

Established in Holland in 1958 as a photo-lab, Souverein has turned increasingly to providing pre-press services to magazines and advertisers, using six Graphic Paintbox systems in its two offices in Weesp and Amsterdam.

Woman

Paintbox artist Audrey van Aarssen created this image from Miriam Jeurissen's photograph. The image was art directed by Erik Krouse for the VSB Bank.

Pig

Art directed by Rijk de Gooyer for the Nederlandse Vegetarische Bond, this image was photograhed by Lex Brand and the Paintbox artist was David Kasperma.

Douwe Egberts Coffee

This advert for coffee
was written by Jan
Ottenhof, art directed by
Chris Leather and
photographed by Paul
Ruitgror. The Paintbox
artist was Karin Spyker,
and the account manager
Don Kouwenhouven.

Shin Yagamishi

This series of twelve images Faces (of which four are shown here) was created for an exhibition by the photographer Shin Yagamishi using the Graphic Paintbox at Sohbi Corporation. They were also featured in magazines in autumn 1992. James Onoda was the model in each case, and the body painting was by Tatsuya Ishii. The images were created on Paintbox by Aogu Kinoshita, under the direction of Hidenori Kataoka. The images evoke a mixture of traditional and modern imagery, with links from Kabuki to Art Nouveau to Body Art.

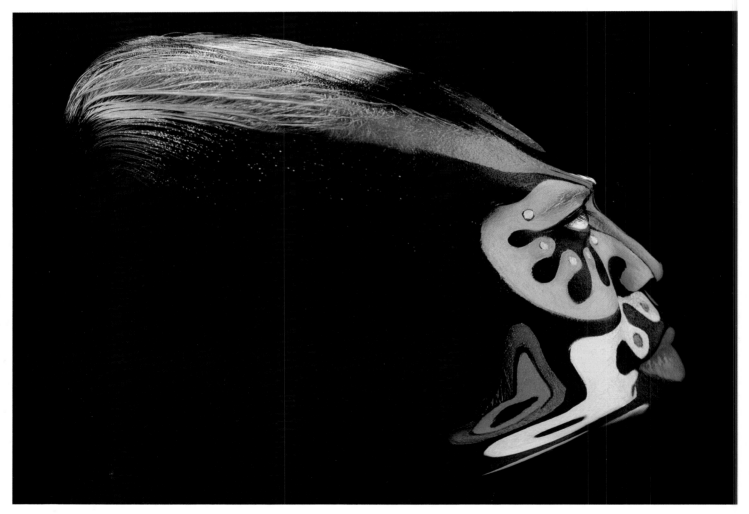

Tape House Design

This New York company, part of Tape House Digital Inc., offers Video Paintbox post-production and titling services for television and commercial users.

Wild

Title from a promotional video for National Geographic, designed and art directed by Phil Price.

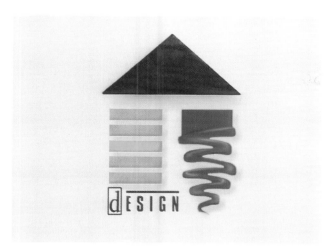

Tape House Design Logo

Art directed by Phil Price,
and designed by Michael
Umon, 1992.

Geraldo

End frame from a TV
promotion created for
Tribune Creative Services,
art directed and designed
by Phil Price.

Tapestry

Based in London, Tapestry's graphic work on Paintbox and Apple Mac has been recognised in several industry awards.

Bike

Designed by John Whillock for his personal portfolio, this racing bike was created entirely on Paintbox, with no original photography.

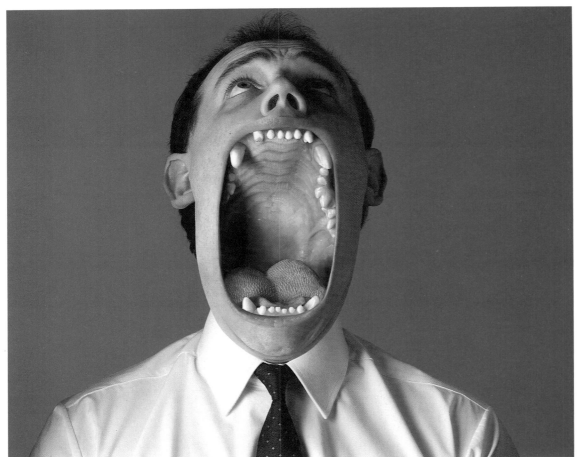

Sculpture

One of two advertisements for Boddington's beer reworked the can into new forms: this one, created in August 1992 for BBH, and art directed by Simon Robinson, with Paintbox designer Raj Taylor, writer Jo Moore and Tapestry's in-house photographer Dennis Watson, won the XYZ Award for Best Press Advertisement of the Year.

Throat Lozenges – Dequacaine

Viv Walsh from BMP,DDB, Needham art-directed this dramatic poster, with Paintbox designer Mark Henry, writer Joe Tanner and photographer Paul Windsor.

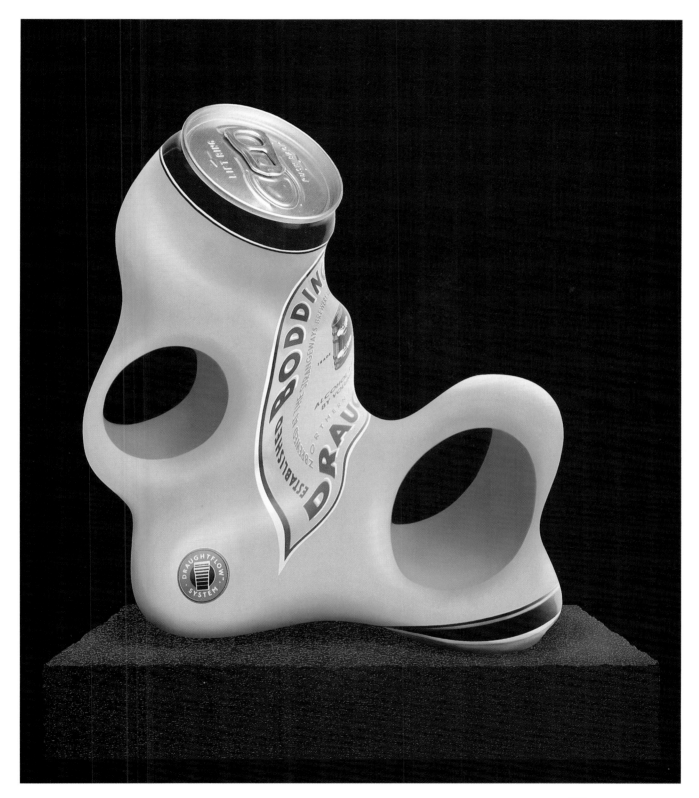

Michael Tiedeman

Michael Tiedeman is Design Director for WCVB-TV in Boston, Massachusetts. He works regularly with the Paintbox for this station, as well as for his own company Nu-Vox. His work has won several awards.

Vote 1992

This telecast tile, for WCVB TV, was designed by Michael Tiedeman with Christine Finn and won a 1992 American Corporate Identity award.

Nu Vox

Animated personal logo, designed by Michael Tiedeman

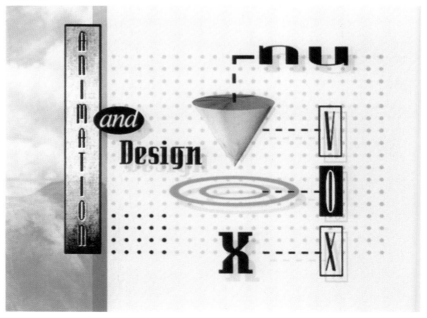

International News

These titles for a WCVB
TV newscast, designed by
Michael Tiedeman, won a
1992 BDA Bronze Award.

Jon Turner

Jon Turner trained at the Royal College of Art and is now head of graphics at Imagination, the London design and communication company.

African Cyberscape
One of a series of illustrations created on Paintbox for the book *The Retail Future* written by Lewis Blackwell and Jan Burney.

Just what makes today's shops so appealing?

One of a series of illustrations created on Paintbox for the book *The Retail Future*, in homage to Richard Hamilton's famous 1956 collage print.

Videosmith

Mark Tatulli, the Paintbox artist at Videosmith in Philadelphia, created this animated sequence as a title for the local television show Floor Talk.

View Studio Inc

Based in Hollywood, California, View Studio provides both video and graphic Paintbox services to a wide range of clients. In 1983 Robert Engelpiepen was one of the first artists to make the transition to computerised video graphics using the first Paintbox system in Hollywood: the studio now has a V-Series Paintbox and a Harry. The animation shown here is a promotional piece for a forthcoming film of Ayn Rand's *Atlas Shrugged*.

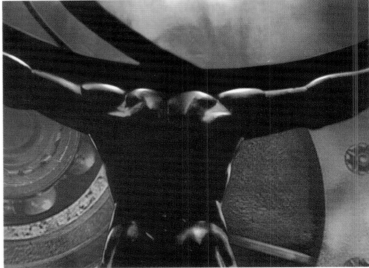

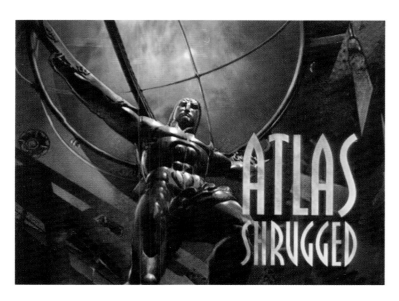

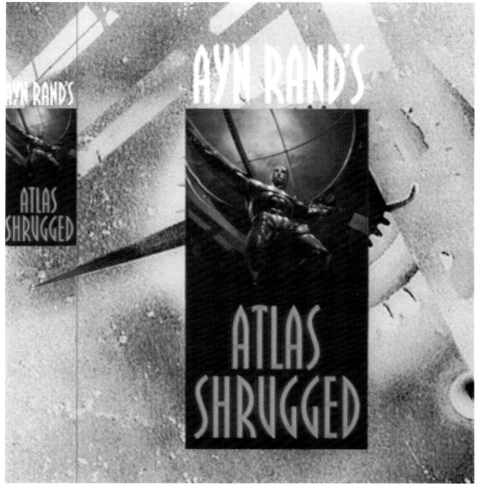

Wiz-Art / Lief Sorensen

Lief Sorensen runs the Paintbox studio
Wiz-Art, in Odense in Denmark.

Fractals

Magazine cover design
generated on Paintbox,
art direction and design
by Lief Sorensen, based
on developing a prism
and spectrum motif.

Fish

Reminiscent in its texture
and forms of the puzzles
of Escher, the image was
created on-screen from
two transparencies.

Watch

Based on Dali's famous   images was designed by
painting, this series of   Lief Sorensen.

Zoom TV

An independent television producer in Barcelona, Zoom has an in-house Paintbox facility, one of the first set ups in Spain.

Culebron con Huerfanito
Culebron con Caballero Inexistante

A collage of images for items on the Revista Visual programme, designed and art directed by Beto Compagnucci, with Paintbox operator Elisa Sauleda. The titles translate literally as 'Snake with litle orphan' and 'Snake with the invisible man', but the Spanish word Culebron is also used in the sense of a serial or soap opera: thus the visual pun.

129

Holger Zeh

Holger Zeh studied at the Royal College of
Art in London where this commercial for the
German-made Space Beer was part of his
diploma presentation. He is now working as a
freelance Paintbox artist in Berlin.

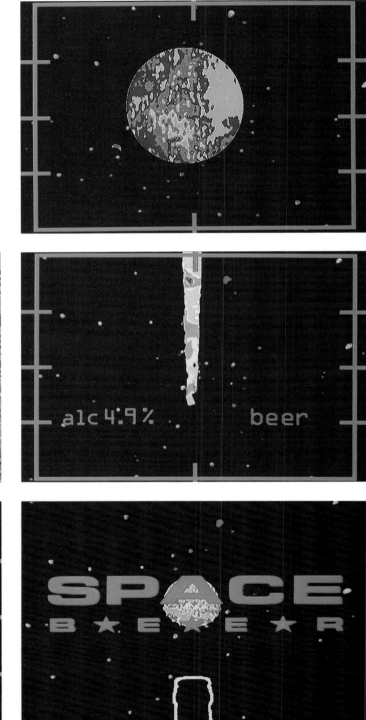

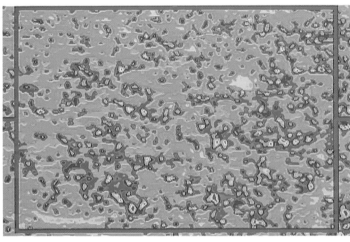

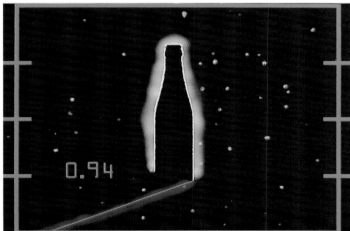

PAINTBOX
THE FUTURE

Bob Pank,
Technical Communications Manager, Quantel

Paintbox was designed to give the television industry the electronic equivalent of a complete graphics studio. This was an area which, it appeared, had been neglected by the new technologies that were sweeping through so many industries in the early 1980s. There had been some attempts at the application of computers to the task but, with their complex operating systems and mediocre picture quality, they had a mixed reception. What was needed was a very much more radical design dedicated to the task of graphics rather than being an adaptation of a general purpose computer. The two areas requiring attention were the processing power needed to create high quality results at the speed of the artist and a user interface that could be both understood and quickly mastered by traditionally trained designers.

The result, the Quantel Paintbox, appeared in 1982. Its development required the best of digital electronic design skills and the application of the latest technology, coupled with an understanding of the needs of the graphics environment and the way designers work. Since then, the Paintbox has found its way into every aspect of television post production, from salvaging damaged or imperfect footage through on-air presentation to high end image manipulation for commercials. The launch of the Graphic Paintbox in the mid 1980s brought the same techniques and creative freedoms to designers working with the printed image, and more recently the Desktop Paintbox has broadened the net to cover the burgeoning professional desktop publishing market. Meanwhile, developments for the television industry had not stood still; Paintbox's role in the production process widened considerably with the introduction of Harry, its intimate relationship with Paintbox allowing Paintbox techniques to be applied to the moving image.

Implicit in the development of television as a communications medium is the central idea of the change from a text-based culture to an image-based one. Television, of course, has not supplanted newspapers, books and magazines. But television's potential for offering information and entertainment in a wholly new way has created new ways of handling images and text. These new approaches, originally unique to television have since spilled over into other media. The use of live action over cartoon graphics is a case in point: another is the use of frame on frame techniques in magazines, and of subtler information graphics and diagrams in newspapers. Technological developments are partly the cause for such developments, but another part is that readers were familiar with such devices from television, and so accepted them.

Paintbox was developed in response to needs in television. In common with many technological innovations, availability created new demands, and led to further applications. Because, in the case of Paintbox, the user interface was highly flexible, the potential of the machine developed rapidly. The increasing complexity and high quality of television and commercial imagery has been facilitated by Paintbox: to speak of Paintbox pushing the development of graphics forward, or being pulled along by them, is to fail to realize that Paintbox is at the cutting edge, and in a simultaneous state of development with graphic and television ideas.

Looking back at the eleven years of Paintbox then, what we see are many developments in terms of applications, bringing Paintbox techniques to bear on a much wider range of tasks, and extending the Paintbox operating philosophy into the realms of editing and opticals. But despite all this change, what has remained constant is the method of working of Paintbox; in other words, the better way of achieving the desired result it introduced has not, so far, itself been bettered. Is this likely to change in the foreseeable future? Of course time will continue to bring a host of new technological changes which can be applied to the processes used for painting, but will they alter the way the Paintbox works? Or, more important, what effect will it have on the facilities available to the artist? It is all too easy to get bound up in the wonderment of the ever increasing power of the silicon chip but that does not automatically translate into practical benefits.

THE FUTURE FOR PAINTBOX

It is only 11 years since the Paintbox first appeared while the history of television production stretches for some 60 years, and the print industry back into the Middle Ages. Put another way, if the life of television were to be compressed into 24 hours Paintbox would not appear until after seven in the evening, while it would be close on midnight in the history of printing. The question is, is the Paintbox a real necessity or just a passing fad?

Being late on the scene does not necessarily mean that the facilities were not required from the beginning. For example the VTR did not become available until 1956, when television was already some 25 years old, and it is still going strong, although it is just possible that it may decline and be replaced by disk or solid state recorders. That makes the point that it is the function of recording that has always been in demand; whether the medium is magnetic tape, disk or silicon chips is immaterial so long as the job is done, efficiently and cost-effectively. As for Paintbox, truth is that graphics were a requirement before Paintbox appeared on the scene – programme makers wanted to use images to explain, entertain, persuade and inform. All that has happened is that the technology has changed: graphics will always be in demand – this bodes well for Paintbox!

At first there was some resistance to Paintbox because it demanded a high capital outlay in an area where budgets had always been based on the cost of art materials and photographic work. It took a while before the value of the equipment became recognized and accepted as being cost effective. The efficiency has never been in doubt; in one experiment, an illustrator attempted a freehand painting of a landscape which he believed would take two days to bring to an acceptable standard. It was completed within two hours on Paintbox.

It is tempting to imagine that new technology will bring a continuous improvement to performance but what should that improvement be – speed perhaps? With current technology the system is able to operate at the speed of the artist: he is not kept waiting for a process to be completed: the system is already very responsive. What it does now it does well, with good quality and in good time. It is more likely that technology will be applied to introduce changes in the range of processes available for the artist to encompass new areas.

TRENDS IN TECHNOLOGY

The technology which is of specific interest to Paintbox design is that of digital electronics. This has been the fastest changing area of electronics over the last decade and there is no sign that the pace is slowing yet. The technology brings new building blocks which, in many cases, perform the same functions as the old ones but are smaller and more powerful yet consume less power, cost less, are faster... often all of these! Sometimes such changes just make it easier or cheaper to manufacture a product and sometimes they step over a threshold and open up new possibilities.

The architecture used and the design of the software also have a formidable influence on the product. The flow of the data must be well organized as must the presentation of the controls. In the limit there is the barrier of the speed of the artist and his use of hand and eye to express what is in the mind. Maybe, one day, there will be a better way to transfer thoughts into pictures but that is not in sight yet. This look at how technological change will affect the Paintbox assumes there will be no radical change in the architecture and software.

Two of the greatest changes that have taken place in methods of construction are ASICs (application specific integrated circuits), and surface mount. Jointly they have compressed the size of the hardware and eased manufacture. At the same time they allow more to be included inside a given box so the possibilities for extending and improving the range of facilities increase as time goes on.

The first Paintbox, the Classic, was constructed from proprietary components, any of which could be purchased on the open market. What made it unique was its design and software. Today the design has been altered in that a number of the functions that took up large quantities of components have been squeezed onto ASICs (application specific integrated circuits). Their use is far more efficient in terms of power consumption and space. Typically one ASIC replaces between 50 and 100 components, may require a tenth of the power and, because it is compact with the parts very close together, can typically operate up to ten times faster. The cost of design and initial manufacture of an ASIC is high so there must be a proven need and a stable design established before the investment is made. It is a measure of the success of the Paintbox that the new design which produced the V-series in 1989 makes wide use of ASICs, a fact that played a great part in the tenfold reduction in size and power consumption over its eight year old predecessor.

Surface mount is a high-tech method of assembling components onto circuit boards. The components themselves are specially made for surface mount assembly and are many times smaller than their conventional equivalents. They are so small that the soldering iron can no longer be used. It is replaced by a machine and the whole process of assembly becomes much more automated. The benefit is that many times more components can be assembled into a given area of circuit and at a lower cost.

RANDOM ACCESS MEMORY

Today most of the RAM manufacturers are Japanese. In this age of digital technology no one appreciates the importance of RAM more, so much so that it has been dubbed 'the rice of electronics', the basic staple of the whole giant industry. In our corner of the industry RAM is extensively used and plays a

The Domino system consists of a lab unit and bench unit (opposite and above) for creating digitally optical effect on movie film.

The trend is for the new components to cost less, use a fraction of the power and work faster. Such changes make it economically viable to add much more in the way of RAM which can be useful in a number of ways. For example images held in RAM can be instantly available both for viewing and for processing. The alternative is to recall them from disk – an operation that takes at least around ´ to one second with standard drives for television images, more for the large files required for printed images. New types of operation can be explored as is seen with the Harriet. This is, in essence, a Paintbox augmented by a video RAM recorder and a host of extra software. The arrangement has led to a great extension of possibilities in the area of animation where fast access to large numbers of video frames is essential.

The development of RAM continues,even if the manufacturers appear to be stuck on their four times tables. As 4 and 16 megabit RAMs become available, their applications will spread as their price comes down. At the moment there is no end in sight to this development – up to at least as far as 256 megabits. That's enough to store around 40 television pictures on a single chip and no less than 4096 times the capacity of the largest RAM chips available in 1980. When such a part becomes economically accessible the applications will spread again. For example it would be quite feasible to build television RAM recorders of an hour's duration. This may challenge the current trend of turning to disks for image storage... if RAM is cheap enough and has the advantage of easy instant access why bother with disks? The answer is of course that disks have been developing too, as we will see. However, it is certainly possible to see RAM enabling huge extensions to the possibilities offered for animation, but it is unlikely that this would greatly change the fundamentals of Paintbox operation for the creation of graphics.

vital part. Throughout operation pictures are stored in RAM chips. For television the size of the data file that makes up a picture is today fixed by the CCIR 601 component digital coding standard, adopted by the production equipment manufacturers to ensure the best quality of pictures thought the production chain. There are two television line standards now in use. 525 line television pictures, used mainly in North America and Japan, coded in the CCIR 601 standard, create files of 700 kilobytes; the others, including Europe, use the 625 line system; picture files are 830 kilobytes. In practice files may be up to 50% bigger when an accompanying mask or stencil is in use. The original Classic Paintbox design employed numerous 64K bit Rams spread over three circuit cards to make up a frame store for a colour picture and its stencil. Eight years on the 1M bit RAM was used reducing the component count for the frame store by 16 fold. In print, with the Graphic Paintbox, the same high density RAM allowed the introduction of the XL 5000 x 4000 frame store version, enabling it to be used for the production of second original transparencies which would withstand enlargement even to billboard proportions.

DISKS

While the silicon chippers have been beavering away to great effect, so have the computer disk manufacturers. There seems to be an unending rivalry between these two arms of the computer industry. Indeed, if one lagged behind it could be expected that the other would seize part of the other's market. After all, to some extent, they are both offering the same facility, digital data storage.

In graphics systems, disks are used as the archive and bulk storage medium for images. With a television picture file occupying around one megabyte and there being a common practical requirement for storage of 200 pictures or more, there was an immediate pressure for large disk capacities. Back at the beginning of the 1980s disks were magnetic, 14 inches across and the drives tended to rival washing machines for power, size and noise! For all that the storage of a fixed drive would be only around 100 megabytes; less for a removable. Paintbox kicked off with a relatively compact 168 megabyte 14-inch fixed model which stood a mere 10´ inches high.

When calculating its next capacities the disk industry is, in turn, stuck on its two times table. At the same time there is a trend to use ever smaller platters. As far as the manufacturers are concerned 14-inch drives have been long forgotten. There has been a progression from 14 to 10´, 5¨, 3´ and 2´ inch diameters to become the basis for the next generation of drives. The result has been an increase in storage density at a rate on a par with that we have seen in RAM.

The redesign of the Paintbox in 1989 was able to use a 185 megabyte drive with 5¨ inch platters which measured under two inches in height. Within three years 1000 megabyte drives with 3´ inch platters have become available. Back in 1989 it was staggering to hear a prediction that by the year 2000 there would be 2 inch drives with a capacity of 2,000 megabytes or more. It did not take long for that to look like a real possibility.

The increase in capacities and shrinkage of size has been accompanied by a tumbling of

the price for a megabyte of storage, the currency of disk drives. The result is that it is now quite practical to store several hundreds of television pictures on a tiny disk inside the machine. Back in the mid 1980s a removable pack containing three 8 inch magnetic platters was received as manna from Heaven by Paintbox users. Each pack had a capacity for some 80 pictures and offered a means of off-line storage and archive as well as transfer to other machines. Despite the cost of around $8 per picture this RSD (removable storage drive) became widely used and a de facto standard. In the television production centres of the world designers could be seen scurrying to their studios with that familiar blue plastic pack tucked firmly under the arm.

New technologies for removable media have been emerging, most notably in the area of optical disks. These are generally very robust and have a high packing density making them an excellent medium for archiving and transfer purposes. Among the first optical disks available were WORMs, Write Once Read Many (times). Although the large capacities were welcomed the lack of re-writability was seen as a distinct disadvantage. At the time of the launch of the Paintbox V in 1989 a new type of disk arrived, the magneto-optical disk drive. This offers full read and write capabilities on its single 5" inch platter storing 650 megabytes, enough for around 700 pictures. Prices continue to tumble but already this system offers storage at less than 25 cents per picture.

Back in the early 1980s picture storage was at a premium but, with some careful management, was sufficient. By the early 1990s the situation had already changed dramatically, to bring bulk storage at an affordable price. Disk technology continues to move forward to offer further advantages in capacity and price but it is of decreasing significance to the designer of still graphics who already has most of the capacity he needs at an affordable price.

One area of disk development that has caused a good deal of interest is in that of disk speed. Although Paintbox admirably fills the role needed for still television graphics, it has something of a strained relationship with live moving video. Obviously it is not possible to paint animations in real time but there remains a very real need to be able to interface with live video. One solution that works very well is to use a large RAM store, such as the ramcorder in Harriet, to act as a buffer between the real time video world of 25 or 30 frames per second, and the speed at which the Paintbox can handle pictures – largely dictated by the speed of its disk system. During the years of the Paintbox's existence this has not changed greatly. Individual designs vary but a general figure would show a speed increase of some 3:1 meaning it still takes around half a second for the disk to load a new picture into the RAM framestore. Meanwhile ramcorders, which can operate at full video speed, have remained trapped by the cost of the necessary chips (itself something dictated by governments rather than the free market economy). So, for the present, economics dictate that the ramcorder stays as an animation store rather than a full edit, or even programme, length store. This is one situation bound to change greatly in the future.

A slightly different approach to the structure of the disk drive led to the development of the parallel access drive. Very simply this means that instead of reading or writing just to one head at a time it can operate simultaneously with a group of heads. These were originally developed for the super computer market but with data transfer rates approaching that needed for real time digital video there was another application too. These developments took place in the mid 1980s and led to the arrival of machines such as the Abekas A60 series of video disk recorders and the Quantel Harry. The latter was introduced with storage for some 2,000 frames (80 seconds of video) with the added advantage of real time random access. Over six years this grew to over 7,500 frames or 5 minutes. Although Harry offered a wealth of other applications for compositing and editing it was also used as an animation store for Paintbox. Today every Harry suite includes a Paintbox – a measure of the importance of the graphics facility in the advanced post production suite. The same drives also made the Graphic Paintbox a viable proposition, where their speed translates into transferring large picture files – typically 60 megabytes – to and from disk in reasonable times.

INTEGRATED MACHINES

The introduction of Paintbox sparked off a revolution. This most immediately affected those involved with television graphics production and it spread from there. Although Paintbox is a graphics studio in a box it is never used on its own. It is always sitting somewhere in a production chain and working in conjunction with other equipment. Its operation with still stores makes up a graphics creation, storage and presentation system. Many edit facilities call on the Paintbox for their graphics requirement. It is useful to have one nearby. Its use with Harry, as a part of the Harry suite, placed Paintbox directly into the editing and compositing environment. It is not surprising that later developments, the building of single machines for the whole

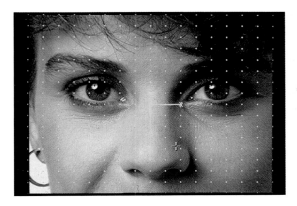

editing and compositing operation, should include Paintbox functions as a part of the system.

In 1992 Quantel launched two new systems, Hal and Henry. The former is dedicated to the operation of compositing, the creation and assembly of any number of layers of video, and the latter is a digital editing system. Both require only the addition of a VTR along with monitoring for pictures and sound to complete the suite. It is a testimony to the importance of Paintbox in these production areas, which are outside the activities of the traditional graphics department, that its functions are included as an integral part of each system.

PROCESSORS

Paintbox is unlike computer graphics systems in that its hardware does not, in general, make use of a computer to process the pictures. The computer processor it has is used mainly in the role of control and system organization rather than image processing, standing Paintbox apart from computer graphics machines. It is purpose built, from the ground up, for the tasks of the television graphics studio. Its dedicated hardware provides the power to perform even the most technically demanding tasks at speeds that keep pace with the artist. At the same time the specification has always called for the very best possible quality, a fact that multiplies the requirements for processing. For example painting which, in computer terms, is very processor intensive, is

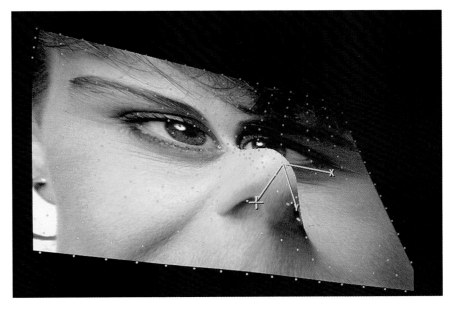

CONTOUR

Contour is the most recent facility available on Paintbox, and extends the range of the machine beyond the conventional graphic studio. Contour allows an image to be spatially distorted. Imagine an image printed on flat rubber sheet: as the sheet is pulled, pushed, curled or wrapped the image distorts with it. This can be used to achieve striking graphic effects (in 2D or 3D) or to achieve practical tasks such as putting a label on a bottle. Contour is also available on Harriet, Hal and Henry to produce dynamic effects and morphing when used with dissolves.

performed by dedicated hardware. Both the width and the type of brush used have a bearing of the processing required, the worst case being the widest airbrush. The aim of the dedicated painting hardware is to keep pace with the artist, even in the worst case. Another function assigned to hardware is that of picture manipulation. Re-sizing and changes of perspective require that every pixel has to be recalculated.

As the size of the image increases so the power of the system needs to be increased to continue to keep pace with the artist. For today's television the size of the picture is fixed but in print there is a very different story. And already there is talk of higher definition for television. The two Paintboxes for print, Desktop and Graphic, handle pictures 16 times and 60 times bigger than those used for television. In the case of the Graphic Paintbox the need for an increase in processing power is reflected in the size of the system but the Desktop Paintbox, designed in 1991, has been accommodated in a box the same size as its video counterpart: a measure of the increased power of the newer technology.

3D COMPUTER GRAPHICS

The output of 3D computer graphics is commonly seen on television. The usual place is for animated logos or, more rarely, as a means to illustrate a story or some technical point. Commercials also make use of the special effects that computer graphics can bring. It has to be said that this has been an area of very great change over the last ten or so years. The change has come about through huge enhancements in the power of the computer hardware and the sophistication of the software. The results have borne the marks of the machines that were used to make them. Earlier popular applications often resulted in the display of wire frame drawings swinging through space... the flying look was popular. As processing improved the frames were rendered and a more solid look appeared although it was often rather obviously constructed of polygons. Today the effects can be far more subtle and can loose that obvious computer look.

Due to the time consuming and complex nature of setting up this type of computer work and the subsequent time needed to process the result (We'll leave that to render overnight) it does not fit with the normal style of Paintbox operation. Also the operators require a different form of training and must be, at the very least, computer literate. Even so it is true that contributions from both types of machines are frequently needed to produce an overall result. With this in mind there has been the development of interfaces to go between the Paintbox and the computer graphics machines. In this way the benefits of each machine are realized to best effect.

In the future both computer systems and the software will continue to develop at a frantic pace. The speed of processing will improve and range of what can be done will grow. 3D computer graphics and Paintbox are both well established and it is now clear that they continue down separate paths. The idea of being able to join them together when needed seems to be the right one.

INTERFACING AND COMPATIBILITY

There has always been the need to join machines together and today's technology provides the best opportunities ever to realize this aim. Certainly the subjects of interfacing and compatibility are close to the heart of everyone considering the acquisition of any new graphics equipment in the television environment. A new type of approach to this has been seen in the building of integrated machines such as Hal, Henry and Harriet where a complete working environment is provided within one box. This obviates much of the need to connect with a wide range of other equipment, usually requiring just a single video source and a recorder to start producing results. In a parallel development for the printing world, the introduction of the Desktop Paintbox to bring creative colour handling alongside the Apple Macintosh's text and line capabilities has now made it possible, after acquisition of original images by scanner, to move from concept to top quality, print ready film separations entirely digitally. Such systems have only become possible with digital techniques. They could never have been constructed in the analogue world.

For Paintbox in television, interfacing is a major subject. Not only is it necessary to connect with the video world but it is also important to be able to exchange images with computer graphics machines as well as still stores and image archives. Looking into the general subject it rapidly becomes clear just how well organized the television world is. Apart from differences of international standards, which are almost entirely covered by a total of only two – the 525 and 625 line systems mentioned earlier – there are very few difficulties in plugging one machine into another. With the advent of digital equipment and the setting of the standard for the interface there is a general move away from analogue in favour of digital connections. The first defined digital interface was parallel (CCIR 656) and required a 25 pin connector and special, costly cable which could not run for more than 100 metres. More recently the serial digital interface has greatly simplified the connection and requires only a single coax cable to connect between machines, just like the analogue days but, with the excellent integrity of digital signals, much better! In the future an increasing proportion of television equipment will be supplied with the serial digital interface.

After looking at interfaces for television, the world of computers has the appearance of chaos. To connect two computers together for the exchange of images there is a host of interfaces using different methods of connection and various protocols. After coping with that there is often no fixed line or aspect ratio standard used. Even then you may still find that the picture is upside down (yes, it happened!). The solution is to use the right interface cards and software to sort out the situation. Then you can connect two machines together. After that if you wish to introduce another type of computer it may

well be that there is another set of hoops to go through. Of course it need not be a nightmare situation but there are plenty of traps for the naïve to fall into. When working between computers and the Paintbox the solution used so far has been to design interfaces for each specific case. It is likely that in the future there will be a greater degree of standardization, especially within specific areas of the industry, so that interfaces can be more generally applied.

Another important area for the Paintbox to interface with is still stores. This is particularly important for a broadcaster who will be operating both types of machine with the Paintbox generating the graphics and the still store being used for general storage and for presentation of the stills into programmes. The Picturenet system developed by Quantel for operation with both the Picturebox still store and the Paintbox has already proved very popular. It provides a means of passing pictures around a network and offers access to ample storage. The network is connected by means of ethernet so that a single coax cable can connect the machines and it is easy to add more. The development of the Picturenet has been a major step and provides ways for system expansion even to a global scale. In the future we can expect to see use made of this so that images can be quickly made available from a wide spread of sources.

Finally there is the question of compatibility. In digital television the pictures themselves all use the same format with the only possible variable being the number of lines, either 525 or 625. The introduction of the Paintbox V in 1989 saw the first use of magneto-optical disks. Since then there has been a policy to make sure that all Quantel machines use a common format and will be able to read and write images on this disk. This has resulted in a range of equipment which can exchange images by disk. This can cut across boundaries of different image sizes, these being automatically converted. Thus, for instance, television images can easily find their way into print, with surprisingly good results, particularly if the images originated on film and remained in the digital domain down the whole imaging chain from telecine to colour separations. In all it is clear that image exchange by interface, network or disk will be of major importance to the future of Paintbox and its ease will continue to improve.

SPHERES OF OPERATION

At the outset Paintbox was intended to perform all the operations needed in the graphics department, a role that it has fulfilled superbly. Operations range from the routines of the daily news, sports and current affairs to projects for dramas, promotional campaigns and commercials. Its ability to add special effects to frames of video were recognized early on. One project involved the changing of the colour of a car in a finished commercial that would otherwise have notched up astronomic sums to re-shoot, the only other path that looked possible. Maybe that was the beginning of its reputation as a fix-it box. But, like Yellow Pages, Paintbox is not just to be picked up when things go wrong!

Paintbox was developed for use by graphic designers and it is indeed mainly them who use it, in television and in print. Its presence in edit suites has led to a few editors picking up the pen to perform the occasional quick task such as to repair a matte. In the print industry, a version of the system optimized for use in the trade shop environment – the Repro Paintbox – has also been introduced. At the same time some designers have grown up with the Paintbox and adapted their skills towards animation, compositing and editing. These people will always make full use of the Paintbox wherever it is placed. Hence the rationale for its being a part of Harriet (graphics animation), Hal (compositing) and Henry (editing). As time goes on the major change will be the continuing improvement in the availability of Paintbox facilities. With that a broader profile of people will come to use the equipment beyond the designers now involved. There are already places where operational staff are working on Paintbox under the guidance of a design director. This does not represent a downgrading of the equipment but a need to spread access to it as its usefulness becomes more widely recognized.

HD TV, WIDE SCREEN AND FILM

There are changes on the horizon for the format of television. There has been much talk and noise at trade shows about high definition and wide screen television. To date it is only the Japanese who have gone as far as staging regular broadcasts of high-definition television but it seems certain that, in time, there will be change.

In Europe there is a proposal to start broadcasts of 16:9 aspect ratio pictures using the PALPlus system. This is seen as a way of being able to get a better-looking picture while still using most of the existing equipment. In production the signal format is the same so the CCIR 601 digital format can still be used. That also means a host of other equipment, including VTRs, can be operated without change. At home your existing 4:3 set will still work but the picture will have some black lines at the top and bottom.

As for Paintbox, it comes into the category of a CCIR 601 user and so will have no difficulty with the signal. To see the picture in the correct way it will be necessary to use a 16:9 monitor. This will, of course, make all the 4:3 originated pictures look fat (for example circles would no longer be correctly proportioned, and text would appear in an extended form), but the real 16:9 images will look fine. Paintbox could be used without alteration, but there would be areas where things could be made a little easier for the operator. Paintbox has the capability to alter the aspect ratio of objects so there should be no long term problem in working with this new format. A change of software would be needed to restore full operational capabilities.

High definition, or advanced television as the Americans like to call it, is currently in a hiatus. While NHK in Japan is making 8 hours a day of 1125 line high-definition transmissions via satellite there is no other regular broadcast. Irregular happenings, such as the Olympics, bring out the world high-definition facilities and wonderful programmes are made, but few can see them. In 1993 there will be a recommendation made to the US government for an advanced television system. What that will be and what impact it will have on existing studio and production equipment is not yet known. It is quite possible that it will call for a higher resolution than that now used. Paintbox high-definition was produced in 1990 to help those working with the new formats. It proved that the techniques used in the standard resolution would translate well into the proposed new television systems. It also made the statement that the Paintbox can be re-moulded into other new standards and will be available for them in the future.

Before the advent of digital television equipment it used to be that the cinema was the place to see the best imaginative special effects. In those days the medium of film offered far more in flexibility for post production. Several Star Wars and Terminators later it is clear that the movies can still carry some spectacular effects but that industry has been looking over its shoulder with some envy at the easy availability of special techniques in television. In 1992 Quantel launched a product to help redress the balance, Domino: Digital Opticals for Movies. This is a special effects platform which allows many of the latest television techniques be applied to film and has many operational similarities to Hal. A major component of that system is the painting facility. As in Hal, Domino has no separate Paintbox as such but the functions are built-in; there is now effectively a Paintbox for film. This is relatively new for this industry but it is sure that the film maker will come to love the Paintbox just as the television and print industries have already. Domino will also enable the producer concentrating on making television programmes for international release to neatly sidestep the issue of varying national broadcasting standards. The production remains on film throughout post production, is distributed on film and only converted to the local standard at the point of broadcast.

DATA COMPRESSION

One of the techniques that has received a good deal of attention is that of data compression and it has been closely associated with digital images. The reason is that images require, in computer terms, very large areas of storage. With the continual advance of digital technology and manufacturing techniques it has become possible to put the complex algorithms needed for compression into affordable chips. The result is that television pictures can be coded (compressed) or decoded (reconstituted) at video rate. The possibilities are enormous. Already some applications are reaching our homes. CDI depends on heavy compression to cram vast numbers of pictures onto a CD. Many believe the future of television transmission lies in compressed digital techniques and the next generation of the domestic VCR may use it too, bringing digital television into the home. But what effect can it have on Paintbox?

Paintbox exists as a part of production. In the production area there is always a need to maintain the very highest standards of quality. Good as some compression techniques are, none are perfect – particularly not those that give the higher data savings! As such they do not have a place in the Paintbox where the quality of any image must be paramount. In any case as time passes the need for compression is receding. Already a sufficient number of pictures can be stored on the system and yet larger disks are already easily available. For Paintbox storage is not the issue it once was and until techniques improve or something else changes it is not likely that Paintbox will have need of compression.

CONCLUSIONS

Open a magazine or switch on the television and pretty soon you will be looking at a picture made in Paintbox. What started in 1981 has grown and developed into a product that is used in television and print around the world. For Quantel it is the cornerstone of the product range and has become an integral, fundamental element of many of its major products. The ideas that were built into the first models still stand up today. Its technology, its user friendliness and its efficiency have endured and given the product a long life.

The future of Paintbox is bound up in the future of the demand for images. The signs are this will grow both because of an increasing appetite for pictures and the emergence of new media to use and deliver them. At the same time technology makes Paintbox easier to produce and so more available.

Uses have spread from the original targeted area of graphics design to encompass editing, compositing, animations and all sorts of special effects, in television, print and now film. The users are still mainly designers but the scope is widening to embrace a broader sector of operational staff. Paintbox artists will continue to be valued for their expertise but they will not be the only ones to use the product as its applications touch all types of programming and many aspects of production.

Digital technology not only allows the construction of higher quality individual products but also gives the opportunity to build much bigger ones; integrated machines that contain whole operating environments. The stand alone product, Paintbox, will continue but there will also be a continuing tendency for the functions to be included as a part of larger integrated machines: Domino, Harriet, Hal and Henry are cases in point. Image makers in the 21st century will still be picking up their pen and addressing the now familiar menus. Although the details will inevitably change the fundamentals will be as they are today. Paintbox will remain Paintbox.

Index of Names

Aarsen, Audrey van 32, 46-47
Adams, Brandon 50
Ad Libitum Trannys 48-9
Alonso, Sofia 23
Altered Images 27, 33, 44-5
Alumi, Jordi 26
Anderson, Heidi 29, 54-55
Aogu Kinoshita 35, 52-3
Asanuma, Go 35
Avenue Edit 54-55
Baker, Richard 34, 89-90
Barr, Kevin 56
Bateson, John 34
Bennett, Daniel 80, 83
Bernstein, Rivka 33
Bianco, John 33
Boortz, Jeff 107
Brauer, Bruce Eric 57
British Sky Broadcasting 60-61
Broom, Simon 7
Brouwn, Bruce 58-9
Bullen, Mark 89-90
Bull, Chris 48-9
Butts, Ken 27
Campos, Jose 80,82
Canvin, Steve 20
Centrol Digital 62-3
Chiesa, Elena 64-5
CIA 20, 42
Coding, Dale 21
Coignoux, Eric 66-7
Conte, Anna Maria 68-9
Critz, Anita 88-9
de Gooyer, Rik 110-1
Denny, Michael 34
Dinnis, Rachel 34
Dorrington, Harry 70
Engelsiepen, Bob 86-7, 124-5
English, Bob 6-9, 70-1
English & Pockett 70-1
Esser, Kristian 72-3
Famiglietta, Ralph Jnr. 27, 33, 57
Finn, Christine 74-5
Flynn, Chris 119
Fossen, Mark 44
Framestore 42, 43, 76-7
Frangia, Francesco 78-79
Goodman, Beth 88-9
Grafi-Image 26, 29, 34, 84-5
Grafx Creative Imaging 80-3
Greiman, April 86-7
Grieder, John 44
Harding, Scott 20, 81
Henry, Mark 116
Hierons, Gary 21, 31
Hills, J.G. 76

Hurley, Owen 104
Hyde, Mark 60-61
IBM 88-9
Imagination 30, 120-1
IQ Videographics 34, 89-90
Israel Educational TV 33
Johnson, Andy 88-9
JSP Post 29, 92-3
Kampa, Flavio 106
Kano, Koichi 35
Kasperma, David 110-1
Kataoka, Hidenori 109, 112-3
Kerner, Water 95-6
Kobayashi, Tadatoshi 109
Koedijk, Bieneke 58
Koerner, Mark 45
Kondrat, Mary 54
Kouwenhouven, Don 110-1
Krebs, Catherine 27, 41
Krieger, Jurgen 22,23
Krouse, Erik 110-1
Laserscan Art Box Studio 24, 98-9
Leather, Chris 110-1
Liew, Caroline 92-3
Lifetime Medical TV 42
Lim, Thomas 62
Lipschulz, Mindi 95
M2 Design 100-1
Madragona, Sam 20, 21, 38
Manarchy, Dennis, 33
Mannes-Abbott, Kim 102-3
Maras, Paula 12, 36
Marlow, Mike 100
Martin, Simon 70
McGhee, Mike 43, 77
Mikros-Image 66
Milbergs, Aida 40
Mill, The 28, 104-5
Moore, Jo 117
Mortimer, Chris 77
Mueller, Brent 44-5
Mueller, Jeff 44-5
Munoz, Genis 23
Nakamura, Masahisa 109
NBC News Graphics 27, 40, 41
Norris, Paul 28
Nu-Vox 118
Ochando, Ramon 26, 34
Olsen, Richard 33
Onoda, James 112-3
Ottenhof, Jan 110-1
Ottenlinger, Reinhard 24, 98-9
Palette Studios 56
Pittard, Billy 106
Pittard Sullivan Fitzgerald 36, 106-7
Pockett, Daryl 71

Pointon, Malcolm 48-9
Pool Video 78
POSH 28
Price, Philip 114-5
Ribalte, Vicky 84
Riss, Micha 100
Robinson, Simon 117
Romero, Juan 85
Saito, Hirohi 108
Sohbi Corporation 35, 52-3, 108-9, 112-3,
Sorensen, Lief 33, 126-7
Souverein 24, 46, 58, 72, 96, 102, 110-111,
Sparks, Tom 105
Splash Computer Graphics 28
Spyker, Karin 96-7, 110-1
Sullivan, Ed 106, 107
Sundry, Michelle 54-55
Tanner, Joe 116
Tape House Digital 95, 114-5
Tapestry 116-7
Tatulli, Mark 23, 122-3
Taylor, Raj 117
Tiedeman, Michael 118-9
Todd, Ruff 64-5
Toyoda, Noriyuki 35
Trebaol, Therese 42
Turner, Jon 30, 120-1
Umon, Michael 114-5
van Motman, Jim 24
Videosmith 36, 122-3
View Studio Inc 124-5
Vigon, Jay 109
Vilaseca, Nuria 84
Ward, Mark 54-55
Watermark 95
Watson, Dennis 117
WB5TV 26, 74-5, 118-9
Webb, Mary 20, 42
Whillock, John 116
Whiteley, Simon 48-9
Wieselman, Amy 88-9
Windsor, Paul 116
Winner Communications 36
Wiz-Art 20, 24, 33, 126-7
Wood, Doug 54
Yagamishi, Shin 112-3
Zeh, Holger 130
Zoom TV 25, 128-9

144